WHAT MESSAGES ARE YOUR KIDS GIVING YOU?

WHAT MESSAGES ARE YOUR KIDS GIVING YOU?

RON WOODS

Bookcraft
Salt Lake City, Utah

Library of Congress Catalog Card Number: 89-61693

ISBN 0-88494-703-3

First Printing, 1989

Printed in the United States of America

Incidents and portrayals in this book are fictitious

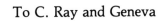

To C. Ray and Geneva

Contents

Preface

A family means communication. Parents and children send messages to one another constantly, some of them clear and purposeful—such as "Here's the mailman," or "Please put out the dog." Others are subtle and unspoken—such as "Nobody appreciates me," or "I want to exert my independence." Among the most powerful, persistent, and often troublesome messages are these unspoken ones.

To complicate matters even further, many of the messages sent by both parents and children are not only unspoken, but also unconscious. For example, a father may feel he is a loving, democratic parent, yet convey "I'm the boss here, and you'd better remember it," in the way he speaks. A mother may love her children greatly, yet be so anxious for them to succeed that she conveys excessive disapproval over minor, childish errors. In both cases, the parents have worthy objectives, yet the messages they unconsciously send will be read loud and clear by their offspring. (Messages from parents to children are covered in my 1987 publication, *What Messages Are You Giving Your Kids?* published by Deseret Book.)

Children also send messages—conscious and unconscious, direct and subtle—beyond the words they speak. Part of them are positive, if unspoken: "I've learned from my past mistakes," "I'm happy to be part of this family," or "I'm learning to serve others." Others are negative: "I don't know how to make wise choices in the face of peer pressure," "I'm burned out and filled with stress," or "I don't care how others feel as long as I get my way."

Parents who ignore the daily messages—especially the subtle, unspoken ones—their children send them, are in danger of failing in their most important task, that of raising capable, responsible adults able to take care of themselves and show concern for others. There are few things more vital for parents than to learn to decipher the messages sent by their children, although a few of them are as difficult to detect and decode as the most sophisticated secret military communications. Only after deciphering can we reinforce the positive ones and intercede to correct the negative ones.

This book considers several such messages, using a story or vignette to illustrate each. While most of these will not match your family precisely, there will certainly be many that will cause you to say, "Ah, ha! Something like that *has* happened in our house. Now I see better what was really happening!" The discussions following each story are generally brief, because once you've recognized the problem, you will likely be stimulated to work out solutions to fit your own family situation.

Human communication is enormously complex, too complex to be mastered in one lifetime. But when it comes to something as important as "reading" our children's needs, we must continually work at it. Our efforts will be rewarded with greater love in the home and greater growth in our children.

1

Help Me Love the Good

A mother regularly reads to her infant, long before he can understand the words. A dad kneels beside his child's crib and helps her with prayer. In these and numerous other ways throughout the child's growing years, parents demonstrate their desire to have their children come to value certain things. Such desires are common to all parents: whatever we call good, we hope our children will also come to value.

Few things in parenting sound simpler than the idea that a child has to be introduced early to those things his parents expect him to later come to value. Unfortunately, it isn't always so simple. Certainly there are no guarantees. Many a reading mother has been chagrined to see her teenager disdain books.

So many factors enter in: peer interests, genetic makeup, a need to be one's own self. Another factor in whether our children adopt the attitudes we value is *how* these are presented to them. A painful statement from a distraught parent is revealing: "I took Jeffrey to church every week; I saw to it he never missed. But now that he's nearly grown, he just won't go. Hates it, he says."

More is evidenced in this statement than merely that the parent valued church and wanted her child to also. There's also a hint about *how* the matter was approached, as if Jeffrey had no choice until he was old enough to put his foot down.

One wonders if an attentive parent would have picked up clues earlier through the messages Jeffrey probably sent that he was not fully accepting his parent's values. Generally, if we're paying attention — as some of the parents in the following stories are — our children will convey to us how they are receiving the things we want them to value.

Don't Make Me Hate
What You Want Me To Love

Mom: "Time for scripture reading, children."
Sue: "Is it a long chapter, Mom?"
Art: "I'm late. I'll miss the bus."
Lou: "Where's my lunch money?"
Mom: "Where's Tom? We need to start."
Art: "He's still in the bathroom. Start anyway."
Mom: "I guess we'll have to. It's Ephesians 6."
Sue: "Is it a long one? I'll miss my bus, too!"
Mom: "No, it's not a long chapter, but if we don't get started . . ."
Art: "OK, then, start."
Mom: (reading) " 'Children, obey your parents in the Lord: for this is right. Honour thy father and

	mother; (which is the first commandment with promise;) that it may be well with thee, and thou mayest live long on the earth.' "
Art:	(down the hall, pounding on the bathroom door) "Tom, get out of there! I need to get in and the bus is almost here."
Mom:	" 'And, ye fathers, provoke not your children to wrath: but bring them up in the nurture and admonition of the Lord.' " (Interrupting herself) "Where are you going, Sue?"
Sue:	"I'm just going to stand at the door and watch for the bus. I'm still listening." (She opens the door a crack and peeks through.)
Lou:	(in a singsong voice) "I need lunch money."
Mom:	" 'Put on the whole armour of God, that ye may be able to stand against the wiles of the devil.' "
Tom:	(coming out of the bathroom, speaking to Art) "Quit pounding the door down and wait your turn."
Art:	"I have to catch a bus, you know. I don't get a ride like you."
Tom:	"Tough!"
Sue:	(from the front door) "I think I hear my bus, Mom."
Lou:	(from the kitchen, shouting) "Is there any change for lunch money? Or do I have to make a lunch, or what?"
Mom:	"Children, for goodness' sake. Who am I reading to? There's not another person in the room. Tom, come here, we're reading scriptures." (Tom disappears into his room.)
Mom:	(hurrying and raising her voice to be heard) " 'Wherefore take unto you the whole armour

of God, that ye may be able to withstand in the evil day, and having done all, to stand. Stand therefore, having your loins girt about with truth, and having on the breastplate of righteousness.' "

Sue: "Yes, Mom, it *is* the bus! I see it!"

Mom: "Wait! Two more verses! 'And your feet shod with the preparation of the gospel of peace;' "

Sue: "I can't wait, Mom. I can't miss it again. 'Bye."

Mom: (rushing now, raising her voice even more at the end as Sue goes out of the door) " 'Above all, taking the shield of faith, wherewith ye shall be able to quench all the *fiery darts of the wicked.*' Oh, and we didn't even have prayers!"

Lou: (from the kitchen) "Why are you shouting, Mom? And what about lunch money?"

If Mom were to spring a pop quiz on her children on the contents of Ephesians 6, I wonder how much they would know about the whole armour of God. Would there be any passing grades?

Timing is everything. And the message the kids are giving Mom this morning is that her timing on scripture reading is way off. She finds herself reading to an empty room and to listeners who are, at best, distracted. Perhaps the fault lies as much with a lack of organization in the children themselves as with Mom's poor choice of reading time. But the effect is the same, no matter whose fault it is.

Mom wants the children to learn to love the scriptures. But they may be learning that the morning scripture reading is at best a nuisance to be ignored and worked around.

If Mom will think about her goals in this regard, she will find a better way. As in so many tasks related to parenting, it isn't only *what* is done, but *how*.

What Is Meant by "Support" of Church Activities?

The monthly ward youth committee meeting was running overtime. The discussion had become lively over the matter of dance instruction for the youth.

"Look," one of the adult leaders, Brother Calhoun, was saying, "It's clear the kids need this. If you've seen how they dance, you'll know. They didn't show up last time because we didn't have the bishop push it hard enough."

Everyone in the room thought back to a week ago Friday night when an instructor had been brought in to teach the youth how to waltz, foxtrot, and cha-cha. The event was anything but a grand success. Besides some of the youth and adult leaders, four teens had shown up, all of them girls.

Bishop Foote turned to the Laurel president. "What do you think, Leeann? Is this something we ought to try again?"

"Well, Bishop," Leeann said, "I don't know. I think we could probably get a few more people out—at least the girls; I never know about the guys—but I'm not sure *anybody* is really very interested."

Leeann's comment gave Tommy Brackett, the teachers quorum president, courage to speak up. "The teachers won't come, I can tell you that. They think it's stupid."

"Not the teachers' cup of . . . uh, Postum, eh?" Bishop Foote grinned.

"I'll say not," said Tommy.

"That's the attitude we have to change, Bishop," Brother Calhoun exclaimed. "If we just tell them we're having an activity and they need to support it, and if we can get the parents on our side, the kids will come."

Tommy shook his head sharply and turned away, but he said no more. There was an uncomfortable silence in the room. Finally, a newcomer to the meeting spoke up. It was Ricardo Valdez, the new leader of the priests. "Bishop, if I could say something." Bishop Foote nodded, and Ricardo began.

"I don't really know if the priests would come. They might, especially if the instruction was attached to a regular dance or other activity. And if we pushed them hard, there's no doubt we could get more of them out. They're good guys, and they'll be supportive if it's what we really want. But I wonder if that's the way we ought to go."

Ricardo paused, and Brother Calhoun started to speak, but Bishop Foote raised his hand slightly, absently waving him off and encouraging Ricardo to proceed.

"Well, my dad always says, 'The church was made for man, not man for the church.' He said it again a while back when we were planning a stake youth activity and trying to figure out how to 'make' people come out. He said, 'If you plan the right activity, people will come. If they don't, they probably didn't need it in the first place.' "

Ricardo is sending an important message—and it is an important one not only for young people but for all of us. Sometimes leaders get the cart before the horse, or the organization before the people. With the best of intentions, church, government, or school planners occasionally provide an activity that few people are interested in, then make them feel guilty for not "supporting" it.

In the Church as elsewhere, we must be careful not to rely on the wrong reason for involving people: presiding authority rather than member need. When we speak too often in terms of "supporting the activity," instead of trying to determine which activities will best support the members, we're taking a dangerous short-cut. It may bring us instant results in numbers attending, but probably very little in the way of long-term member growth and development.

As parents, we're anxious to make sure our children grow up involved in the activities of the Church. We're justifiably concerned when a child sleeps too late for Church meetings or demonstrates in some other way a lack of motivation. But by failing to point out the differences between basic meetings we're directed by commandment to attend, and the multitudes of non-required activities—no matter how well planned they may be—we run the risk of causing a child to feel so much coercion that he rejects the whole package and ends up disliking what we want him to like.

Don't Push Me Too Hard

The family knelt around the dinner table and Dad said, "Would you say the prayer, Markie?"

Five-year-old Markie said, "I don't want to."

Dad's first inclination was to say, "Markie, when Dad asks you to say the prayer, you need to do it." But he thought better of it, patted Markie's back a couple of times, and said, "All right, if you don't feel like it today, maybe you will tomorrow. I'd like to say it this time."

This small incident illustrates an important issue. A parent often faces a difficult decision as to the "cost" of pushing a child into a particular behavior. In this instance, Dad and Mom clearly would like Markie to learn to participate in family prayers. When he doesn't prefer to, they are faced with questions like these: If we don't help him learn at an early age to say the prayer, will he find it harder later on? Should we force his involvement at an age when we have considerable control over him or let him make his own decision? If we let Markie "get away" with not taking his turn, will the other children decide they don't want to participate either?

These are valid questions, and each situation may have different answers. But one key issue stands out: if Dad sees Markie's refusal as a message of challenge to his parental authority, he will probably handle the situation wrongly. On the other hand, if Markie feels his preferences are accepted, his expanded self-esteem may actually lessen any future anxieties about participating.

Even if Dad does feel his authority threatened, a quiet discussion *after* dinner to discover Markie's feelings will be more productive than an on-the-knees confrontation at the moment. The goal is for Markie to come to see that saying the prayer is a privilege rather than a duty. Such a lesson will likely carry a lot more long-term value than one which says, "When Dad asks you to do something, you'd better do it."

Help Me Be Happy

Dora sat in bed, writing in her journal. She wrote:

"What a great day! My thirty-fifth birthday! I'm supposed to feel depressed about 'getting old,' I hear. So far, it hasn't hit me.

"Mom and Dad called early this morning to sing to me, the reading group ladies took me to lunch at Dalton's, and Newell and the kids cooked dinner. Then there were presents to open. Matt had hurried home after school to make a cake—his first—with the help of Betty Crocker. Not bad for an eight-year-old. It was a fun day.

"But the biggest surprise of all came tonight at the concert of the fifth-grade orchestra. Tracy had pestered me for days, asking if I was coming. I kept telling her we were, but every day she kept asking. Tonight, I learned why she was so anxious.

"First, she kept looking at me and grinning so hard she could hardly blow her flute. She would try to pucker, then she'd grin. It was hilarious. I finally had to stop looking at her, for her sake. I didn't think much of it, since she's always such a happy child; I just thought she was glad to have us there.

"We had finished applauding the last number on the program when the music teacher announced that they would now perform a special number. He stepped off the podium. At that, I was startled to see Tracy stand up and head for me! She came, grinning the whole way, got me by the hand, and pulled me to stand up beside her as she directed the orchestra in 'Happy Birthday.' I was amazed!

"She'd arranged the whole thing when she noticed that her concert date was on my birthday. The conductor said he just couldn't refuse her when she came to him so excited. What a girl!"

"Always such a happy child." What a message for a parent to receive. There may be more important things in a child's life than finding and radiating real happiness, but there can't be many! Real happiness is a good sign that things are going well—and that they will likely go well for the rest of her days.

Dora's thrill at Tracy's public surprise probably elicited from her a profusion of thanks and praise, both of which will help Tracy want to continue her efforts at bringing happiness to others—efforts that are probably major contributors to her own happiness.

Teach Me to Serve, and to Like It

"This has been a wonderful meeting so far," Brother Hobbes said as he stepped to the microphone. "We know, of course, that many of you would be here anyway, but we also thank those who came long distances or who came out especially to hear what Geneal has to say at her farewell. I'm anxious, too! But I know it will be good."

The packed meetinghouse was attentive. Brother Hobbes went on. "Geneal, or Hermana Hobbes, as they will call her in Peru, is a wonderful daughter—and I'm not prejudiced. I don't know a person more oriented toward service and helping other people than Geneal is and has been throughout her life.

"I remember an incident years back when she must've been in about the seventh grade. I guess I'm not a very modern, liberated man, folks, because I confess that my wife, Lily, has always made my lunch for me to take to work, and I've always been glad to let her. Her sandwiches are just plain better than mine, you know.

"Well, one morning Lily wasn't feeling well, and the family knew it because she'd been sick the night before. I was getting up when this same little Geneal, who's now going out to serve in the mission field, asked me quietly, so as not to wake her mom, 'Dad, do you want me to make your lunch?'

"Well," Brother Hobbes said with a touch of emotion, "I couldn't believe it. I want you to know that I managed to handle this one the right way, I think. I went over and hugged her and said, 'Honey, that's the nicest thing anybody's asked me all day. Thanks very much, but I can do it.' Then she said, 'I got up early so I could.' 'In that case,' I said, 'I'd love you to.' "

Brother Hobbes did handle it the right way: he praised his daughter for her efforts to serve and make others happy. By so doing, he probably reinforced in her a desire to continue serving. Geneal didn't become so oriented toward service and helping other people by accident. She found pleasure in it, and part of the pleasure came from being praised and recognized in her early years, so that service became second nature to her.

A few people learn so early about helping others that they appear to have never actually needed to learn it; they seem to have been born that way. But it probably isn't true. Even they undoubtedly had to learn to serve.

This is comforting news to parents who have a child who is *not* a natural at service, the one whose specialty seems to be more toward the selfish end of the scale. It's comforting to know that praise, encouragement, and sincere appreciation for even the smallest acts of kindness can turn a child more toward service, especially if started soon enough. Only through this kind of reinforcement will a child learn not only to serve but also to enjoy it.

Help Me Care about What Others Think

"Mark, we've talked for some time now," Carrie Pope said. "Your dad and I understand your feelings, I think, and you understand ours. You know we were very upset to find the note on your bed this morning telling us you weren't going to the cabin. And you know our concern wasn't only because you didn't go. A fourteen-year-old has a right not to have to go on every outing the family takes, but the way it was handled — with you disappearing so we couldn't talk about it — that was the problem. I understand now you felt like we wouldn't listen, and you had to do it that way. Still, it wasn't right. We almost didn't go because we didn't know where you were, but decided not to ruin it for the rest of the family."

Carrie and Doug had spent over an hour with their son discussing this incident, and all were more relaxed now than at the start. The living room was getting dark, but no one had yet turned on the lights.

"There is one other thing we haven't talked about," Doug said.

Mark looked at him. "What's that?"

"It's how the others in the family felt. Mark, you know we'd talked about this trip for weeks. Everybody made an effort to be there. Sandra took a day off work, and Adam missed a class. They did these things of their own accord when we said this might be the last time Grandpa could ever get up to the cabin. Who knows how mobile he'll be after his surgery?"

"That's a point," Carrie added. "Everybody put a special effort into going because they thought we were *all* going to be there. Then when we found your note and you were gone, there were some reactions. Want to hear them?"

Mark hesitated before answering. Finally, he said, "I guess so."

"Well, without mentioning names, certain of your siblings thought you were being pretty selfish. Others seemed hurt. I don't know if you can understand that, but put yourself in their place. After putting themselves out to make it a whole-family outing, then to have you drop out at the last minute without discussion — well, it left them feeling sort of cheated. Do you think you should do something about their feelings?"

Parents have to be concerned not only with the messages their children send *them*, but with the messages they send *others* as well. In this case, Mark breached an understood contract with his parents and with his siblings. They feel wounded not only because of his decision but because of his method of dropping out of the trip and out of sight. He owes them an apology.

This morning, Mark cared only about himself. By this evening, he probably has a broader perspective. The experience will help him realize that one of the most important things in life is caring about the feelings of others. If parents handle these incidents correctly, they have a chance of instilling in their children a concern for others that will guide their actions throughout life.

Winning at All Costs?

"Brethren," the stake president said as he stepped up to the microphone, "before we divide to go to our various sections of today's stake priesthood meeting, I want to read you a letter. I think you of the Aaronic Priesthood will be especially interested in it, but I want the older men to hear it, too."

President Cox pulled from his inside jacket pocket a folded sheet of paper. "It's from one of the basketball officials who officiates in many of our stake games. Here's what he has to say:

Dear President Cox and Counselors:

I've officiated at stake and regional basketball games for over 27 years now. I suppose you could say I enjoy it.

I've noticed, over the years, that the competition has become keener in many wards than when I started. The spirit of fun has often been replaced by an attitude of, "If we don't win, it wasn't fun." I hate to see this, but it does seem to be a trend.

However, I want to point out a positive example in one of your wards—the Twelfth Ward teachers-age team, coached by Brother Dean Mathis.

I'd noticed when I refereed games with this team how they seemed different. And I started asking questions. One of the boys told me that on the Twelfth Ward's team, every player gets equal time on the floor. Win or lose—and they win quite a few—the boys know they will have a chance to make their contribution. Brother Mathis has one of his younger children keep track of playing time and advise him when it's time for a player to go in or come out.

I know a father of one of these boys who claims his boy never was interested in Church sports until they moved into the Twelfth Ward. The boy isn't very good at basketball, and in his previous ward he was made to feel that he wasn't needed on the team. Here, he says he's never felt this way. He recognizes he's not the best player, but he gets as much play time as anybody else.

I've also overheard Brother Mathis talking to his players during time-outs. One of the most remarkable things I ever heard in Church sports was when he asked them to let a certain player on another team (who seems a bit handicapped) have a clear shot or two, next time the ball came to him.

I thought you'd like to know I think this man is the type we need more of in Church sports programs if we want our youth to come to value fair play and sportsmanship.

Sincerely,
Roland Akers

"Brethren," President Cox went on, as he put the letter back in his pocket, "I hope we take this message to heart. I congratulate the Twelfth Ward and Brother Mathis—and all others who go out of their way to remember and teach what Church sports is all about—for their fine work.

"Sometimes I really wonder about us. I was at a Cub Scout Pinewood Derby race not long ago in one of our wards. I couldn't believe the attitudes a couple of the boys displayed, until I saw how their dads were acting! Then it was obvious. These men came close to blows! And all over which one of their sons' puny little wobbly-wheeled wooden race cars would go down a track faster than the other."

President Cox shook his head, "Brethren, we must do better."

For sure, winning is fun and losing isn't. But some things matter more than winning, and some things matter less than losing. At certain ages, kids need help with these concepts. Such concepts may not seem natural at first, and they will need constant repetition. But kids can get the message, just as Brother Mathis's team did.

Of course, words alone won't do it. A coach who talks about playing for the fun of playing and then gets tense in a close game and yanks out all but his best players will erase with his actions the value of his words. A parent's sideline diatribes may convey to his children something more than healthy competitive fervor.

Teaching our children to care about others, even under conditions of stress and competition, will be one of the most important virtues we can instill.

2

Help Me Grow and Change

One of the ironies of parenthood is that we claim to want our children to grow and develop, yet at the same time we often instinctively resist the changes required in such growth and development. Something within us — perhaps the realization that the maturing of our children means a parallel aging of ourselves — causes us at times to want to keep things as they are.

The trouble is that our natural parental need to "hold on" runs right up against a child's natural need to get free. There are occasional moments of noise and harassment when parents envy the "empty nest," but most of the time we like our children around. All the while we try to hold on to them, their destiny inexorably pushes them toward abandoning the nest.

Growth and change are necessary for them to realize their potential as adults. We must help them in all the little steps along the way, and when the time is right we must not only let them go but also help them be prepared to do so—perhaps even to push them a bit. This means being observant of the messages they send us in their fledgling efforts to fly on their own—messages like those in the following vignettes.

Help Me Feel Trusted

"Danny, you're coming up too fast . . . Danny!"

Darrell's words were lost in the confusion as his son swerved the car out around the van that was rapidly coming to a stop in front of them. Before Darrell could say anything else, the car was headed for three pedestrians in a crosswalk in front of the van. Fortunately for them, they scampered to the sidewalk, leaving only dirty looks behind them as Danny coasted on through, a chagrined look on his face.

"Good night! Danny! You could have killed those people," Darrell said. "You can't just swerve out around a driver who's coming to a stop." He caught his breath and went on. "You have to assume he has a reason for stopping—like pedestrians—and that whatever made him stop will soon be in the other lane, too."

"I didn't know it was a crosswalk, Dad," Danny said.

"I know that, but it's your job to watch out." Darrell went on for quite a while, getting more upset by the minute as he thought about what could have happened, while Danny drove silently the rest of the way home. He seemed contrite and a little shaken, but Darrell wanted to be sure the point was made. His closing line was, "You've had your license for only a few weeks, but you won't have it much longer if you keep up this kind of stuff."

When they got home, Danny went straight to his room until dinner. Darrell followed him in and said, "I have to be able to trust you to be safe, Danny. Until I can do that . . ." He left the sentence unfinished.

"I know, Dad," Danny said.

Later in the evening, Darrell answered the phone. It was Jeremy, his younger son, ready to be picked up from his part-time janitorial job at his uncle's barber shop. Darrell saw Danny watching him from the dining room table, where his homework was spread out. Ever since getting his driver's license, Danny had been looking for chances to drive and had been the one to pick up his brother from work. "OK, son, I'll be down." Danny looked away quickly.

As he went down the hall to the bedroom for the keys, something told Darrell that the question of trust was a critical one for his relationship with his son. When he came back, he went to Danny. "Here, son," he said, holding out the keys, "Why don't you pick up Jeremy?"

Darrell has decided to risk trusting his son. Since the incident today was isolated from Danny's regular good driving patterns, and since the boy appeared sufficiently humbled by the experience, why not? A week or two without practice won't likely teach Danny to drive any better, anyway.

There are key situations where trust needs to be shown. Dad is reading the message that it's time to let Danny grow. It seems likely the boy will better remember the trust shown than any lecture given or restrictions applied.

One of parenting's difficult decisions is when to extend trust after a breach has been made. If withheld too long, children come to feel they are personally untrustworthy, that *they*, rather than certain of their *actions*, are the problem. And, as is the danger with other self-esteem deficits, such views can become self-fulfilling.

Accept Me

Arlene drove home slowly tonight, confused and hurt. She couldn't believe what had happened. Only two months into a job she loved, she'd been fired. It wasn't fair.

Only the second real job of her life, waiting tables might not be especially glamorous, but Arlene loved the chance to meet people and the challenge of helping them have a good time eating out. A good tip was the frosting on the cake; being friendly and attentive was her real joy. And for a part-time job while she went to the community college, Arlene thought waitressing pay wasn't half bad when tips were averaged in.

Yet tonight Mrs. Adamson, the night supervisor at the Breadbasket, had let her go. Oh, it was clear why, and she had been warned before, but still, some of the times she'd been late hadn't been her fault. And recently she had been doing better. If only Mrs. Adamson could have waited another week or two, she would've seen.

But it was too late now. There was nothing to be done.

As she drove, Arlene thought of what lay ahead. Besides looking for another job, she had to decide how to tell her friends—a few of whom she'd recently been telling how much she liked this job.

One thing was clear: telling her parents would have to wait. She was in no shape emotionally to face that.

She knew already what they would say. Mom would say, "Arlene! How many times did we tell you, bosses won't tolerate lateness!" or another version of the same speech. Dad would only shake his head and click his tongue, but the message sent by those gestures was the same rejecting one he'd always given.

Arlene had seen it before when she got a poor grade or made some other mistake. Her parents didn't tolerate "I-told-you-so's" from anyone else, but they each had their own way of communicating them to Arlene. When she'd protested that certain things were out of her control, she still felt rejected.

No, telling Mom and Dad would have to wait. First, she would talk to Cally, her best friend for the past five years. Cally would understand.

Arlene's folks haven't been reading very well her message of "Don't reject me." In fact, they thought they were helping her by communicating that *they* knew all along she'd lose her job if she kept on being late. They probably did know it, and they turned out to be right.

But at the moment, what Arlene needs is acceptance. She needs her parents to commiserate with her and to help her feel optimistic about her future prospects. It's a necessary growth step. *Then,* after that, there may be a time when she can hear their reminders about employers who won't tolerate repeated lateness, especially in a new, untested employee. This is another kind of growth step, but it can only have value if it comes *after* the acceptance step.

Even better, when Arlene feels her parents' support she may mention her error herself, in which case they will need do no preaching about it whatsoever. She has probably learned the lesson well by her own hard experience.

Parents who aren't careful about conveying support and acceptance run the risk of alienating their children and driving the older ones prematurely out of the home, sometimes into early, immature marriages which often prove faulty as a replacement for the acceptance not found at home.

Help Me Overcome My Fears

Sacrament meeting was close to starting when Ted leaned over to Lois. "Where's Mike?" he asked.

"I don't know," she said. "He's nervous about his talk, you know. He told me this morning he wouldn't give it."

"I thought he had it all ready," Ted said.

"Oh, he does. He's just scared. You know how he is in new situations."

Ted rose and went out of the chapel doors just as the bishop was standing up to start the meeting. Following a quick circuit through the hallways and restrooms, he cut across the cultural hall. Only one bank of lights was on, and Ted had moved halfway across the hall, certain his search was futile, when he saw his son. Always big for his twelve years, Michael now looked strangely small and vulnerable as he huddled in a corner beside the big accordion-fold door separating him from the meeting under way on the other side.

Ted stifled his inclination to chastise his son for not being in the meeting, and when he saw Michael's white face, he was glad he hadn't said anything.

"I'm sick, Dad," Michael said pathetically. Mike had a way of looking as if he would faint or vomit at any minute, and even though his parents knew that most of his "fear-illnesses" came from mental rather than physical causes, the queasy stomach was still real enough.

"You don't look too good," Ted said lamely. When his wait for Michael to speak produced no results, Ted went on. "Because of the talk?"

"I don't know. Probably."

Ted looked at his son. Mike was obviously suffering. How often Ted and Lois had seen this happen with Mike when he faced new things: the first day of school each fall, scout camp, swimming lessons. Even when the activity was one Mike really wanted to do, if new surroundings or people were involved he would freeze up at the last minute and make himself sick.

At first they ignored it, hoping the problem would go away. Then they tried talking Mike out of it. Sometimes Ted had simply pushed him into the activity anyway; often this worked, and within a few minutes Mike was fine.

Ted wondered if that was the approach he should take now. He could probably bully Mike into walking into the meeting with him and point him toward the front. He would likely do fine once he got up there. But what if the boy actually became sick on the stand? Or if he stood up and couldn't speak? Maybe these weren't likely, but they were still possible, and was the risk worth it? What would such a devastating experience, especially in front of his peers, do to a young person?

Carefully, Ted said, "What about the talk, son? Do you think you can give it?"

"I don't know, Dad. Maybe I can do it another day."

Again, Ted stifled his inclination to point out that next time Mike would likely feel just as he was feeling this time, and said instead, "Will you do that?"

"Yes."

"You'd have to tell the bishopric you're sick today, but would like another chance. Are you willing to do that?"

"Yes."

"Then I'm not worried. You'll do fine. Now, come in and sit down." Ted put his arm around his son's shoulder and they walked into the chapel.

Two weeks later, Ted and Lois watched anxiously as Mike sat on the stand, as pale as he'd been in the cultural hall. But when the counselor conducting the meeting announced him as the youth speaker, Mike stood and spoke clearly, gaining strength as he went, and even smiling with the congregation at one of his own humorous comments toward the end.

Ted's response was likely the proper one in this case. While Michael may have a way to go before being able to function normally in new situations, he has taken a big step forward in accepting the idea that all of us face difficult situations at times. He will grow by facing his fears.

All of us—children and adults—have fears. But it turns out that adults don't often understand what kids fear the most. While most parents are aware that teens are greatly concerned with peer approval, studies made in 1988 show that this concern starts much earlier than commonly thought—in fact, as early as kindergarten. Look at the following concerns of elementary school children:

—Repeating a grade is rated as worse than facing major surgery.

—Visiting the school principal's office is ranked as more stressful than visiting the dentist.

—Getting a bad report card is considered worse than getting lost.

There is a common theme in each of these fears; the reason children apparently consider them so troubling is that they involve a fear of peer ridicule, something adults are prone to underrate. "It doesn't matter what others think," we say. But to our kids it *does* matter, and a great deal. In fact, few things matter more. Wise parents will pay careful attention to those messages from their children which indicate fears, and particularly those concerning peer rejection.

Give Me Space

Lorraine opened the front door of the house and watched her son Jared get off the junior high bus.

Jared looked startled. "Yeah, I brought it," he said without her even asking, as he brushed past her and up the stairs to his room.

Uh oh! Lorraine was sure she'd been too aggressive, and wished she'd played it cooler. Jared had a stubborn streak and could be pushed too far. But this wasn't just *any* report card. Well, she would let it go for now. As much as she wanted to, she didn't follow Jared upstairs.

Soon, he was back down for his so-called after-school snack—actually more like a full meal of toast and peanut butter sandwiches. She noticed how he casually dropped his report card on the table on the way to the refrigerator. Just as casually, she went to the table and leaned over it.

She bit her tongue at sight of the first grade: a D+. Well, at least it was passing. All the other grades were C's or better. "Jared," she said, "this is *good!*"

"Sure, Mom." He looked at her while he chewed.

"Well, not exactly *great*, you know," she said, "but a lot better than what we might have had, right?"

"Right," he said with a tiny grin and an effort at disinterest.

Lorraine was greatly relieved to see all the grades were passing. That was a lot better than last time, when Jared had brought home three Incompletes on the midterm report. It had been a long nine weeks, especially the last month, with weekly reports from teachers outlining missing and failing work to be made up. Lorraine had tried everything to get Jared interested in getting caught up. "Don't worry, Mom, I'll make it," he'd say. But obviously he was not putting in any real effort.

And then, in the last week of the term, Jared came down with a bad case of bronchitis. On medication, he missed the whole week. After getting Jared's commitment that he would do the work, Lorraine had made two trips to school to pick up work, had also corrected work sheets, supervised encyclopedia research papers, and proctored tests, then made another trip to take everything back to the teachers in time to be graded. In spite of his commitment, Jared had protested more than once that there was too much, that he didn't understand the math, and that it was too late. Lorraine had insisted he meet his commitment and assured him that each teacher had said he could still pass if he turned the prescribed work in on time. Sometimes she felt she was pushing almost to Jared's limits, but she'd stuck with it. And it had worked.

"You know you could have done a lot better, don't you?" Lorraine asked.

"Yes, but I started late, you know."

"What about this term? Are you going to keep up, now that you've caught up and seen you can do it?"

"Yes, I am."

"That's great, Jared. And like I told you last week, I'm going to back off now and let you work on your own for the most part."

"For the most part?" Jared asked.

"Well, I'm still your mom, and I can ask you how things are coming and expect an answer, can't I?" Jared didn't answer, but Lorraine could tell he had no argument with that.

"Also, Jared, it's good that you want to do better and have committed to do so. I hope you've learned that it's easier to keep up than to catch up. But you still need a plan, a system, so you won't fall back into old habits of postponing work. After dinner let's talk about a plan. OK?"

"OK."

Lorraine might be logically justified in keeping the pressure on. But she knows her son's limits and realizes there comes a time to let him take over on his own. Last week wasn't one of those times, but this week probably is. At the start of a new term, Jared deserves a chance to show he's learned to do a better job.

Any other course of action would come out of Lorraine's fear, and she's wise to put her fear on hold momentarily. She still has time to let Jared put his plan into action before the first parent-teacher conference of the term.

Children do often grow and learn from the lessons we teach them. But sometimes we have to back off and give them some space before they will demonstrate in their own way what they've learned.

Notice When I Improve

"Dad, I changed a long time ago. You just never noticed until I won the fireworks."

Jill's bitter comment ended the short conversation she'd been having with her dad. It had started when Dad had noticed a big package of fireworks in her room and asked her about it. "Looks like you're ready for the Fourth, Jill. Where did you get all these?"

"From the *Examiner*," she said.

"Oh? What for?"

"For being paper girl of the month," she said.

Dad was clearly surprised. "Oh!" he said. "Well, good, honey. Uh, what about complaints?"

"Dad, I haven't had a complaint for six months."

"You haven't?"

"No," Jill said. "I haven't been late or anything for a long time. I know I used to be, but I made a new year's resolution to do better."

Dad could see that Jill was hurt or frustrated. "I didn't know. I just remember you were pretty sloppy with your route for a long time. I guess I didn't know you'd changed your ways."

That's when Jill said the words that ended the conversation. "Dad, I changed a long time ago. But you never noticed until I won the fireworks."

Dad has missed something important here. He still thinks of Jill as a sloppy paper girl, yet she's been exemplary for six months. Why hasn't he noticed?

There is no excuse. It's just that parents are often slow to notice new messages their children send them. Old views and labels die hard sometimes. No wonder kids get discouraged in trying to please us.

It's ironic how we strive to cause our offspring to act in new ways, then fail to note the changes when they occur.

Two things will help. First, we have to be more observant of the changes and growth made. Next, we must *tell* them we've noticed. Instead of always watching for the negatives and commenting on those, why can't we do better at noticing and mentioning the positives?

3

Help Me Become Independent

A three-year-old screams, "I can do it myself!" At dinner, an eleven-year-old pushes her plate away and announces quietly, "I don't like meat loaf, I have never liked meat loaf, and I'm never eating it again." A four-teen-year-old at a party stays out later than allowed. A sixteen-year-old states he isn't going on the family vacation this year.

Independence: it's one of childhood's greatest desires. Kids everywhere look forward to making their own decisions, being free of restraint, and being in control of themselves. We who are now parents experienced similar feelings and frustrations in our own quest for independence. But our memories are sometimes short. Now, as we watch our children suffer through their own strivings for independence, we say, "Was I ever like that?"

By properly reading the message kids send about wanting independence, parents can help make the transition from childhood to adulthood smoother. Wisdom and patience are required. Holding on too long can be as harmful as allowing too much freedom too soon, and one of parenthood's most difficult questions is: How do we keep our children safe from situations they can't yet handle while still giving them practice in exercising their free agency?

In these following examples, children send various messages about independence, which their parents—ready or not—must interpret.

Give Me Practice at Making Choices

"How could this happen?" Jan asked herself for the thousandth time. Her eyes were closed, but no sleep had come tonight. Last time she'd looked, the luminous green numbers on the clock-radio read "1:37." Beside her, Jim had finally slept, but fitfully.

Jan had been over it all so many times, but she could make no sense of it, and the hurt was like a wound in her heart. How could Anna, her most obedient, loving, cooperative, helpful child, be led so quickly into a life of drugs, cheating, lying, and deception?

It would be easy to blame certain of Anna's new friends at junior high school, or society in general, or inattentive teachers, or parents too naive to notice the signs until they were blatantly obvious. Yet even if these elements all contributed, was it that simple?

Jan thought back on the good times, the sweet times, when Anna was her old self, her "real" self—as late as last summer on the trip to the coast. Even at twelve, Anna was a good helper, quick to see what needed doing and to jump in and give a hand. The image of her at the overnight stops helping to set things up in the trailer before joining her little brother and sister at play was strong in Jan's mind. She was always so anxious not to disappoint her parents in any way and to be seen as an adult. Maybe too anxious, it now occurred to Jan. Of course, Anna had always been praised for those very traits.

When Anna was younger, for example, Jan had leaned on her heavily for babysitting and chores. She'd wanted her eldest to learn to work, and Anna was unusually willing. If she ever showed any reluctance, Jan would manage to bring her around, then always made a point to praise her in front of the rest of the family, her friends, and church groups. On a few occasions, Jan had intimations that Anna was ridiculed somewhat by certain peers in the neighborhood as being a goody-goody and a mamma's girl. But Anna didn't seem to mind, and Jan didn't concern herself with what others thought.

Now, what in the world had gone wrong?

One of the paradoxes of parenthood is our great desire to have our children always say *yes* to our requests of them, combined with our equally great desire to have them learn to say *no* to certain requests from their peers.

Jan's anxiety is deep and heartfelt. It would be cruel of us to blame her or her husband for Anna's difficulties. Yet perhaps we would find it difficult to blame Anna fully, either.

Jan's memories reveal clues as to possible causes of Anna's being lured into following negative peer influences. She sent her folks some pretty clear messages, actually. She was, for instance, "always so anxious not to disappoint her parents in any way." *Anxious* is a strong word here, and could imply more than a normal desire to please. Even Jan now recognizes that her daughter was "maybe too anxious."

Why would this be so? Again, we can't be sure from the brief view we've had, but there are clues, the first being that Jan "leaned on her heavily." In itself, this isn't necessarily a problem.

But what happened if Anna ever showed any (natural) inclination not to always be helpful? "Jan would manage to bring her around." Could this imply manipulation and an unnaturally strong parental control?

Our last clue is Jan's praise of her daughter's help in spite of peer ridicule. Although Anna "didn't *seem* to mind," it's very possible she actually came to mind a good deal and made a flip-flop to be accepted by her group.

It's in Anna's "old" self, therefore, that we find the potential seeds of her present difficulty. The whole problem could be seen this way: Since Anna had "always" desired to be seen as an adult, yet was perhaps not allowed to make the normal choices to help her become one, she hadn't developed the strength to say no to her friends when she should have.

It's worth noting that our children need to start saying no earlier than we might think. Youth of a generation ago (today's parents) were offered their first drink at an average age of seventeen or eighteen. Surveys show the average age for that first offer today is eleven and a half.

If our children are to learn to say no to undesirable things, they must get a lot of practice. During that practice, they may choose differently from what we would have, but it's the long run we're working toward, where their frequent practice will benefit their quest for autonomy and independence.

Let Me Use My Free Agency

"Sit down, Gwen," Mrs. Carter said, motioning to the couch in her music room. "I like to know something about my students, so before we get started let me ask you about your piano background. You say you used to play?"

"Yes, Mrs. Carter, I'm twenty now, and I haven't played regularly for years, but I started lessons when I was eight and finally quit when I was thirteen. And it's a good thing I did."

"Oh, what do you mean? Most people who take up piano for the second time express regret about the lapse."

Gwen shook her head. "Not me. If I hadn't quit when I did, I'm certain I wouldn't be sitting here today ready to start lessons again. I know myself well enough to know I'd have rebelled. Actually, I had done so mentally already. For months I'd told my parents I wanted to quit lessons, and they would come back with 'You'll be sorry if you do,' and all the things most parents would say. I'm sure I'll say the same thing to my own kids someday! But I wasn't practicing at all and Mom was getting on me all the time about that. I was really hating it.

"So one day, I decided that would be my last lesson, no matter what. I didn't say so to my folks, but that night at home after the lesson, I said, 'I can't stand piano anymore.' We talked a long time, and finally my dad said, 'You'll have to decide.' I said OK, but of course I'd already decided. So the next day I told them I was going to quit.

"If they'd forced me somehow to stay with it, I know things would have gotten worse and I'd have quit to spite them later. As it was, I was totally relieved to be rid of piano. I didn't touch it for ages. Then, one day about two years later, I was bored and I picked up one of my old books and tried working out a piece or two. It was actually fun! Since then, I've bought music and played just for fun. I've recovered a lot of what I'd lost, and now I want more lessons.

"I know I've lost a lot of time. But in my case, I'm certain I wouldn't be here now if I'd been forced to stay with the piano another year back then."

Whether Gwen's parents let her quit piano because they got the message she was sending at the time or for some other reason, her new teacher is hearing it loud and clear: Gwen has now come back to music because she wasn't forced to stay with it at an earlier age.

Some of the most difficult decisions parents have to make involve how much to push for what the parents feel will be good for a child, and how much to let the child decide. There are no clear precedents. One adult points out how glad he is that his parents held his feet to the fire in playing the violin or finishing his Eagle Scout requirements. Another never touches the instrument again or burns his Scout awards because he feels he received them only because of pressure from others rather than because of proper motives on his part. Another regrets that his demand for freedom from practice and discipline kept him from completing worthwhile things.

It's a tough call for a parent to make, and it can't be done in a knee-jerk fashion. It will require careful thought, observation, and discussion. Certainly not in every case does a child respond as the parent predicts when he says, "You'll thank me someday." As with all stock answers and formulas, this one only covers a percentage of the situations.

What About My Need to Prove Myself?

Vivian stood in the entrance stairway of her home, looking down at her son. "This is getting us nowhere, Duane," she said, shaking her head. "You throw this up to us every time you're upset with your dad and me, and it isn't fair."

"And I guess it was fair for you not to let me work when I wanted to!" Duane retorted. The young man was near tears, and since he was nearly eighteen and hardly ever cried anymore, Vivian knew the depth of his feeling was extreme.

"Duane, for the hundredth time, you were barely sixteen, and you were not doing well in school at the time. Yet you wanted to wash dishes until two in the morning on weeknights! How can you think we could allow such a thing? You'd have made a disaster of school."

"Two in the morning? Sure. The job was until about eleven, three nights a week, Mom, and maybe till midnight or one on Fridays and Saturdays."

"That's not how I remember it," Vivian said.

"You can remember it any way you want, Mom, but I *know*. I was the one offered the job, remember?"

Vivian didn't know what else to say. They'd been over this issue many times before. Duane had wanted to work at a job that, in the best judgment of his parents, wasn't compatible with high school. Maybe they'd been right, maybe not, but they'd done their best. "I'm sorry, son. That's all I can say."

"You're sorry you didn't let me take the job? Or sorry I won't see it your way?"

"I don't know. I'm just sorry you feel this way."

"Humph. Well, that's why I'm not so hot on a job for the summer. You wouldn't let me work when I wanted to. Call me a bum if you want, but I'm going to play this summer."

Vivian and her husband made a decision that turned out to have long-lasting effects. Of course, had they allowed Duane to work, it's possible the results would have been as bad or worse. No one can know now. But it's obvious the boy hasn't forgotten that he wasn't allowed to make an adult decision at a time when *he* felt he was ready to do so. He sent a message about needing to prove himself that wasn't accepted by his parents.

Looking back, Duane's folks might wish they had done otherwise, yet at the time, they could only do their best. How could they know how things would turn out, and that almost two years later, their son would still hold against them a decision they made for his own good? The question is how they might have better handled the matter.

If Duane's parents could go back and re-do their decision, they might consider bringing Duane into the decision to keep it from appearing—and being—arbitrary. "What do you expect will happen to your grades?" is a good question to begin with. Next, you can add a contracting question, "Shall we plan out now what will happen if your grade average drops below a B?" This way the parent isn't the villain if things don't go well; reality is.

Praise Me for My Choices

Nine-year-old Alysa ran in the front door and found her mother typing at the home computer in the dining room. "Look, Mom, what I got."

"What, honey?"

"Look at my ears!"

"New earrings! Where did you get those?"

"At the pharmacy, just now. I went with Quinn when you sent him to take back the video. I had some money, and I saw these the other day. They're green, so they'll match my new church dress, won't they?"

"Well, I think they might."

"Quinn said they were ugly and too cheap to be worth anything. But I only had a dollar and a half, and these were in a sale box for ninety-nine cents plus tax. Are they ugly, Mom?"

Mom looked at the plastic clip-on earrings. They were obviously cheaply made and would probably not last a month before the clasps broke. And while they weren't ugly, they weren't exactly attractive either. Overall, they weren't bad, especially for ninety-nine cents.

Mom hesitated an instant before saying, "Honey, if you like them, they're fine. It's your money, and you have to learn to make your own choices. Don't worry about Quinn. Fourteen-year-old big brothers aren't great judges of little girls' jewelry."

Mom hugged her daughter. "Let's get out your dress and see how it matches."

Mom had a choice, and she made the right one. If she were dealing only in objective economic facts, as Quinn was, she might have told Alysa the earrings were likely to break easily and really weren't all that attractive. But she wisely sensed that Alysa was sending a self-esteem message. She was learning to exercise her own judgment in matters of spending money and choosing what she liked. What she needed most was what she got: parental support.

Possibly in a few years, Alysa might look at her cheap green earrings—if they last that long—and find them childish and maybe even ugly. But for now they're just right—because she chose them herself and because her mother reinforced her right to do so.

Choices are good for children. Evidence indicates that toddlers who are given choices show higher academic ability in school. From the infant's dilemma over whether to run through the sprinkler or play in the sandbox, through a youth's choice of which earrings to buy, to the college junior's pondering over majors, minors, and career possibilities, our children send us messages about wanting to make choices and become independent. Parental praise will help them gain confidence in the process.

Give Me Permission to Make Hard Choices

Larry and Sonia sat with their sixteen-year-old son Taylor in the family room. "Son, we've probably talked about this matter long enough," Larry said. "Why don't I summarize your view and you summarize ours, like we usually do, so we can be sure we understand each other, then we'll have to come to a decision and wrap things up?"

"OK," Taylor said.

"OK, you want to go skiing with Jake on Sunday. You know we don't do that kind of activity on Sunday in our house, but Jake is your best friend and in his family it's no problem. You don't feel you'll get into a habit, this is a one-time thing, and so, you say, it can't hurt much. And you also feel you're old enough that you ought to be able to decide on your own. Are we fair to your position?"

"Yeah, I think so," Taylor said, "except to remember the reason for this trip. Jake's dad is here from California, is leaving Monday, and he's not here very often, so he wants to take Jake. He doesn't usually go on Sunday either, but he feels like his dad will be hurt if he doesn't go.

"Now, for your side: you and Mom feel like Sunday shouldn't be used for this sort of thing—ever. You don't like me missing church, and you're afraid I'll get into a habit. You also say that if you let me decide, you don't want to have to face the same question again this whole season."

"OK," Sonia said. "What do we do now?"

No one spoke for a few moments, then Larry said, "I have an idea. Jake is a good kid. Why don't you call him and tell him our concerns and see if there isn't some way to work things out differently? If you'll do that, I think we can let you decide what to do."

Taylor looked doubtful, and Sonia added, "Sounds good to me. It can't hurt to check, Taylor."

Taylor stood up with a sigh and left the room. It was obvious he felt his parents were making too much of a small matter which ought to be his alone to decide. When he came back in the room, he said, "We talked about it and decided we could go to Jake's ward first —they meet earlier—and then go up the canyon."

"That would be better," Sonia said.

"I know it doesn't solve everything in your minds about Sunday, but we would at least get to church."

Who's to say if Larry and Sonia made the right decision in letting Taylor make his own decision about skiing on Sunday? Some will say there is *no* place for such activity. Others, that an occasional excursion doesn't hurt, especially if church is attended first.

Other parents say the important element is simply who gets to decide. Taylor is sending the strong message that he ought to be able to make this choice himself. If Taylor's parents want him to learn independence — as he himself wants — they have probably taken a wise course in giving him permission to do so.

Larry and Sonia were wise enough to get something out of the deal too. They made it clear to Taylor that letting him decide this once meant they wouldn't have to hear similar questions often. While in a petitioning mood, he agreed to their request.

Taylor's parents refrained from "laying down the law." While Taylor may do something they would not prefer, this is probably the kind of situation on which they can safely let him practice his decision-making skills. It's even possible that, after a day on the slopes, he will return closer to their side of the argument than he now is.

While Sonia and Larry could keep Taylor from going this time, there will come a time in a few years when they will have virtually nothing to say about his activities. Better to permit him a certain amount of latitude now, especially in a controlled environment where he may learn that church is the place to be on Sundays.

From Time to Time, I Need to Test the Waters

The afternoon sun streamed across Professor Bormann's desk as he worked on entering the day's quiz results in his grade book. When that was done he'd be on his way home, a little early today, for a family picnic up the canyon. The phone rang at his elbow.

"Bormann here," he said.

"Your wife here," Barbara Bormann said, in an imitation of Jack's deep rumble.

"Hi," Jack said. "I'm about finished, and I'll be along shortly."

"I thought I'd tell you now so you'd have time to think it over before you got here."

"Oh, oh!" Jack said. "The last time you used that line, Jenny had wrecked the car. The time before that, somebody'd spilled a quart of paint on the carpet. Before that . . ."

"I know," Barbara said. "Fortunately, this time it isn't so serious. But your first reaction might not be too happy."

"OK," Jack said, putting down his pen and leaning back in his chair. "I'm ready."

"Well," Barbara started, "you know you've taken Jason over to the church parking lot to practice driving several times?"

"Yes."

"Well, he asked me an hour or so ago if I could drive him over there to practice, but I had piano students."

Jack snapped, "He'd better not have driven down there himself. I told him never to do that."

"He didn't exactly drive, Jack. That's what I'm telling you."

"Go on," Jack said, puzzled.

"Well, he and Clint *pushed* the little car down there."

"Pushed it?"

"Yes. They practiced driving in the lot, then pushed it back."

"For heaven's sake, Barbara. What if somebody had smashed into them on the road? I know it's only two blocks, but we'd still be liable if anything happened."

"I know, dear, I know. I didn't know they'd gone until I saw them pushing it back. When I went out to ask them what they were doing, they said you'd said not to drive on the roads without a license, and that's why they pushed it. I'm afraid I thought it was kind of funny!"

Young people seeking independence will find ways of trying parental patience quite frequently. It's a message parents need to get used to receiving. Whether or not Jason and Clint have made a serious breach of trust or a relatively minor one in this case isn't the point for our purposes. The question is how parents should react to unexpected and creative efforts at independence.

Perhaps by the time Jack gets home he will have devised a method of approaching his boys that won't encourage behavior such as today's but will not come down unduly hard on it, either. A commitment to avoid moving the vehicle in the future—with or without the motor running—in the absence of a licensed adult ought to be sufficient. In time, Jack will probably even come to see the humorous aspects of the incident. If this is the worst his enterprising boys do to test the waters, he will be a fortunate parent indeed.

I Will Often Seek Parental Blessings on My Choices

"McClain, I think we'd better reconsider this deal with Marlo."

"And what, Peggy? Give in? Let her stay?"

"Give in, no. Compromise, maybe."

"What did you have in mind?" McClain asked, using the remote control to turn down the volume on the TV. They'd been in a state of distress for the last twenty-four hours after receiving a phone call from Marlo, their nineteen-year-old daughter, who was clear across the country. She'd left three days before for a supposed week-long Christmas visit to her boyfriend, Pete, and his family; the family had sent her the ticket. Then, somehow, they or she or somebody had found a way for her to stay a few months while Pete got ready for his mission. They knew of a job they thought she could get. Marlo had been excited at the prospect when she'd called last night. Peggy and McClain had not.

Their questions were many: "What about school? You're already registered for winter semester. What about your job here? They're expecting you back. What about living in the same house as Pete and the dangers of too much contact?" The list went on, yet nothing had dissuaded Marlo. She saw nothing but good in the idea.

"Well, here's what I'm thinking," Peggy went on. "We know the problems, and we think it's not wise; but we also see some advantages—living away from home for a while, taking a break from school, etc. We've talked about those.

"However, I believe I read a message in Marlo's tone last night. I think it came awfully close to: 'I'm staying anyway, but I'd really like your blessing.' "

"Well, if she thinks . . ." McClain started.

"Now, wait a minute," Peggy said. "She didn't say that; I just read it from her way of talking. I may be wrong. But if I'm right, it seems to me we have two choices: One is to stick by our guns and say, 'Come home.' She might do it, but the cost might be high in terms of resentment. She might not do it, in which case the cost might be higher, in that she would have had to break with us, defy us, disobey us openly. Neither of these appears worth it to me.

"So, I'm saying, our second choice is to allow her to stay on a few of *our* terms."

"Such as?"

"Such as, we say to Marlo, 'Look, you know we're not happy with your plan and that we feel left out, having to make decisions long distance. But if you want our blessing, you can stay on two conditions: One, you must not live with Pete's family. That's too close for comfort. You'll have to find a nearby family to take you in, in return for housework or babysitting or something. Second, you can stay only if you get the intern job. If that doesn't come through — and it isn't likely — then you mustn't stay and take any old job. That wouldn't be worth missing a semester of school for.

"I think she'll see this as a concession on our part, and unless I miss my guess, she'll see these two requirements as reasonable. I still don't like the thing, McClain, but I don't see any point in forcing a break at this point. She's so excited to stay, and she's past the age where we can say much to force her back if she doesn't want to come. And we stand to push her into an unnecessary break with us. I'm trying now to look at the positive aspects of the experience and to get our input heard."

Peggy has read an important message in her daughter's call. If her interpretation is correct, she and McClain face a vital decision: whether to get part of what they feel is important — or risk getting nothing at all. They're meeting head-on the difficult question: If a child is going to exert her independence — at an age where she has every legal right to — should the parents compromise and try to maintain a degree of input, or should they force a total break?

It's a tough question. In certain situations there might be no possibility of compromise, but those are rare. In most cases parents are able to help their child grow into independence by maintaining as much influence as the child is willing to accept and by giving their blessing to the child's right to choose. The worst mistake is standing so firm as to push the child from the home before she is really ready. Who is helped then?

4

Help Me Learn Responsibility

Studies indicate that modern parents place high on the list of attributes they wish their children to learn, the following: ability to think for themselves, initiative, and acceptance of responsibility. This is interesting in light of similar lists from the 1920s which emphasized obedience, conformity, and respect as the three main traits parents of that day wanted in their children. Look at the change here: in sixty to seventy years, American parents have moved from wanting children to *follow* (conform and obey) to wanting children to *lead out* (think for themselves, show initiative, and accept responsibility). This is a major change in emphasis—perhaps even a revolution!

Now, does the new viewpoint mean these same modern parents want their children to disobey and purposely fail to conform—to *reject* the attitudes of earlier days? I doubt it. All of us want our kids to respond to our wishes (obey) and to more or less follow our views of acceptable standards of behavior (conform). So it's not a matter of one or the other. We needn't toss out the values of the twenties to achieve the values of today. It's a matter of emphasis and balance.

The older values may have an initial appeal to many of us. They sound safer. They would seem to keep our children out of trouble. We tell them what to do—out of our store of wisdom—and they do it, and they're safe. And there's reason in this—but only to a point.

The world has become a complex place. Good employment, for example, generally requires a great degree of responsibility and initiative. We want our kids to learn how to succeed. Perhaps the old values *alone* aren't sufficient to ensure their success in the modern world.

Another way to look at it is this: the obedience we want in a two-year-old, to keep him from running in the street and from throwing dishes, may not be precisely the same type we want in a young adult, who needs to learn to make her way in a world that will reward her for thinking for herself and accepting responsibility for her actions. It's well to remember that, ultimately, we're not raising children but adults. Those traits we hope for in a mature adult must be inculcated in youth.

In the following examples the parents sometimes struggle to read the messages their children send them about their desires to be responsible for themselves.

Let Me Experience Logical Consequences

The phone rang on Mel Cutter's desk. "Sales. May I help you?" he said.

"Mel?"

"Hi, honey," Mel said, recognizing his wife's voice.

"Well, it finally happened."

"What happened, Trish?"

"Garrett lost his paper job," she said.

"Fired?" Mel asked.

"Yes, his supervisor just called me."

Mel sighed. "Well, we can't be surprised about it."

"No, I'm not," Trisha said. "But I wish he could have pulled it together."

"Me too. But he can't be too shocked, either."

"No, I'm sure he won't be. He doesn't know yet. The supervisor wants Garrett to call him as soon as he gets home from school."

"OK, honey, thanks. He has to learn, you know."

"I hope he does. OK, 'bye then."

" 'Bye now."

Mel hung up the phone and leaned back in his chair. Memories came to him of the many times Garrett had been sloppy with his newspaper delivery over the last several months. It was an afternoon route and close to home, which meant Garrett had plenty of time to get off the school bus and get his papers rolled and bagged and still have plenty of time for relaxing and fortifying himself with an after-school snack before starting to deliver. But for days and weeks on end, Garrett would start late. A few customers would call to complain, then the supervisor would call, and Garrett would do better — for a day or two.

He was also consistently late with collecting and paying the publisher, and there were other signs of sloppiness — not bagging the papers in wet weather, lack of care in placement. He'd been warned, and now the boom had been lowered.

Mel doubted if Garrett really cared that much. He didn't seem to care whether or not he lost the job. Each time there'd been a complaint, Garrett had blamed the customer for being too demanding—"fussy" or "cantankerous," he called them.

Mel wondered if they'd done the right thing in letting the problem remain mostly between Garrett and his supervisor. Other than regular reminders to get started on time and occasional observations that eventual termination was probably inevitable, Mel and Trisha had stayed out of it. They'd talked to Garrett more than once about the likely consequences of his poor behavior, then they'd pulled out. Mel hoped there was a lesson for his son in the experience.

Accepting responsibility for oneself includes accepting the results of poor work. As parents, we often want to shield our children from these results. We don't want our children to suffer things like being fired from paper routes. And yet, one of life's most important lessons is that consequences do follow our actions.

Some parents go through years of protecting and bailing out their children. While none of us can judge a situation without knowing all the circumstances—which we never will know, unless it involves us—it's a safe bet to say that too much bailing out doesn't work. A child who is saved and protected and bailed out too often may never learn to accept responsibility for his own life.

Garrett may or may not learn a life-changing lesson from losing his paper job. But he is sending a message which isn't a healthy one: his view that customers who expect their paper to be on time are "fussy" or "cantankerous." He is missing a major point: that of his own responsibility.

Mel and Trisha can help at this point by carefully and gently helping Garrett recognize his own culpability. If Garrett can accept that *he* should have done better, instead of blaming the supervisor or the customers, there's a chance the effect of the logical consequences of his poor work won't be lost on him.

Stand Behind Me

Marvin came in the door from a Church leadership meeting and went to find his second son, who was in front of the TV. "Tom," Marvin said, "I was just visiting with Karl Tobler. He said you were going to call him last week to set up a time when you and he could do your home teaching."

"Oh, yeah, I forgot," Tom said, glancing away from the TV for an instant.

"Well, now there's a problem."

"What's that?" Tom asked, this time taking both eyes from the screen.

"Karl says you're a great partner, but he does rely on you to call him."

"I know, Dad. I just forgot this time. I'll call him tonight."

"But here's the problem, son. Karl got a last-minute work assignment. He's leaving this afternoon for an out-of-town trip, and he'll be gone past the end of the month."

Tom looked at his dad. "Oh," he said.

Karl waited, but Tom was looking at the TV again. After a moment, Karl asked, "What do you think you should do about the home teaching, Tom?"

"What should *I* do about it? What do you mean?"

"Well, son, you're a home teacher to three families. Your companion isn't able to make it this month, partly because you didn't call him on time. I just wondered what you thought you ought to do about it."

"Now, Dad," Tom said, in his light-hearted way, 'I'm nothing but a little ol' sixteen-year-old junior companion. Brother Tobler is the high priest. He's in charge. What does *he* want me to do about it?"

Marvin debated whether to give Tom a lesson on the responsibility of junior companions but decided to skip the lecture and be more direct. "So you think you ought to let your three families go this time?"

Tom looked at his dad, and Marvin decided a little humor might help. "Oh, it's probably OK. I imagine if a cyclone rips the roof off the Burtons' house or one of the Smiths' kids runs away or the Tomlins decide to fall away from the Church this week, they'll call you, won't they?"

"Dad, don't be *too* dumb," Tom said with a suppressed grin. When Marvin didn't respond, Tom added, "I take it you think I ought to find another partner and go home teaching without Brother Tobler."

"What do *you* think?" Marvin asked.

'I think you're the high priests' group leader, and you'd probably do a real good job as my partner."

'I'd be glad to try," Marvin said with a smile.

"And you want *me* to make the appointments, right? And probably give the lesson too? And tell them why Brother Tobler isn't with me? And that next time I'll set up the appointments quicker?"

"You catch on quick, young man, for being, as you say, 'nothing but a little ol' sixteen-year-old junior companion,' " Marvin laughed. "I'll help in any way you want."

"Which means," Tom sighed good-naturedly, "I'll do all the rest, but *you* give the lesson."

"You got it!"

Marvin has made clear who he thinks ought to pick up the reins for the home teaching visits. And Tom's message is, fortunately, one of acceptance of responsibility.

Marvin could have handled the matter differently. He might have come home and announced he was filling in for Karl Tobler and then have simply taken Tom along as his partner to make the visits. But Marvin was wise enough to use the opportunity to teach an important lesson. Fortunately, Tom was willing to accept the responsibility—as long as his dad was supportive and willing to stand behind him.

Sometimes parents expect too little of their children. Other times, they expect too much. It's good to remember there is a middle ground, a supportive sharing of responsibility that allows growth and only gradually moves the parent out of the picture. The amount of sharing needed varies with individual children, and one of parenting's greatest challenges is to discover how much or how little support to give in specific situations. The general guideline is that kids seldom will take more responsibility than we expect them to.

Better Late Than Never

It had been a hectic Saturday, and Silvia was glad it was coming to an end. She was tucking in the baby when she was called to the phone. When she hung up, she immediately went to find nine-year-old Teresa, and located her in her room.

"Teresa," Silvia said, "that was Sister Betham."

"My Primary teacher?"

"Yes." Silvia waited.

Teresa looked at her, puzzled. "So? Why are you looking at me?"

"I'm wondering if you know what she wanted."

"No, I . . ." Suddenly, Teresa's face changed. "Oh," she said, "A talk. I was supposed to give a talk tomorrow. Oh, no! I forgot."

Silvia bit her tongue. She remembered another time when Teresa had forgotten an assignment in school or church—she couldn't remember which just now—and when Teresa had remembered at the last minute, Silvia had not reacted well. She had fussed and fumed and demanded to be told sooner if she was expected to help. The evening had ended with Teresa in tears and her mom frustrated. Later, she'd realized that her actions had probably done little to help Teresa want to accept assignments or to ask her mother's help with them.

This time, Silvia decided, she'd do better. While the last thing she wanted to do tonight was to stay up working on a talk, she could see from her daughter's face that she was upset at having forgotten—and perhaps also upset that her mother was likely to be agitated. Yes, this time, Silvia thought, I will be in control, helping, rather than hurting the situation.

"OK," she said, "Where do we start? Any ideas for a subject?"

Silvia has learned from her past mistake. Instead of *reacting*, she will *act* to make the situation better. She knows she has a choice: she can label Teresa irresponsible for forgetting her talk, or she can increase Teresa's responsible behavior by showing her it's really not too late to prepare a short Primary talk tonight. Her daughter's future acceptance of responsibility may depend a great deal on how such instances are handled.

Parents can model behavior that indicates that a person who takes charge—even if later than preferable—can get a great deal done. Or they can model hand-wringing and teeth-gnashing, but these don't do a lot to help our children become responsible and may even have the opposite effect.

Encourage Me to Take Charge

"Look how big your hands are," Angela said, as she pressed her palm up against her dad's at the dinner table.

"Well, sure, compared to yours," Bill said. "After all, mine have had forty-four years to grow, and yours only eleven. Mine should actually be four times bigger, shouldn't they?"

Angela laughed. "What's this scar on your thumb? Did you suck it too hard when you were a baby?" she teased.

"Not quite, smartie," Bill answered. "Didn't I tell you about how Mister Thumb met Mister Power Saw when I was about your age?"

"No."

"Well, I was at my cousin Gary's house. His folks were gone, and we were cutting wood, just for fun, on a table saw."

"What's that?" Angela asked.

"Like the one Grandpa has in his shop. With the round blade that comes up out of a flat metal table. I'm sure we weren't supposed to be using it without anybody around, but Gary was more than a year older, and he knew how to use it. I'd never been around one, and I didn't know you were supposed to push the last of a narrow board through with another piece of wood. So I used my thumb. Get it now?"

Angela shuddered. "Did it hurt bad?"

"I suppose," Bill said. "I don't really remember that, but I remember I was plenty scared, and it bled pretty good. The cut was kind of jagged, so it scarred."

"What did you do?"

"The main thing I remember is how Gary took over and acted like he was a doctor or something. He walked me into the house, squeezing my thumb to slow the bleeding, then he put me on a bed on the porch and went and got a bandage of some kind to wrap it in. He even put a pillow under my feet—so I wouldn't go into shock, he said. I don't suppose the problem was quite *that* serious, but he said I looked pale. We just waited until his folks came home. I remember having a nap while I waited, so maybe I was kind of shook up."

"What did they say? Did you get in trouble for playing with the saw?"

"I imagine Gary's folks were kind of scared when they saw a trail of blood up the sidewalk to the house. But I don't remember getting in trouble. I guess we'd probably learned our lesson without anybody telling us. What I do remember is how, after they heard the story and checked me over, they praised Gary for keeping cool and taking over like he did. I think he liked hearing that."

I'm sure Gary did enjoy hearing that. Parents who are wise enough to notice and praise the taking of responsibility, rather than always finding fault with the problem, do a great deal to encourage better behavior in the future. There's undoubtedly a place for pointed reminders about the use of dangerous tools, but at the moment praise and support for those things that were done well are vital.

Yet many of us have the tendency to jump right on the cause of the problem: "If you hadn't been playing with things you weren't supposed to touch . . ." or "If you'd been driving under the speed limit . . ." or "If you'd kept up on your homework . . ." These come out of our natural fear that our children will be harmed, but they leave our children feeling as if we haven't even noticed the good things they've tried to do to fix their original mistakes. "Why try?" is then a justifiable but unfortunate conclusion for them to reach.

Teach Me to Handle Money

"Hi, Mom," Alisha said, meeting her mother at the door. "Here's a letter from Bart that came today."

"Oh, great," Jaci said. "He's doing pretty well, isn't he? To write home every week since he got in the MTC, I mean. I didn't know if we could count on him for that." Jaci went to the dining room table and sat down to read. Alisha followed her.

"Yeah, but you're not going to like everything he has to say this time."

"I'm not? What's wrong?"

"Oh, nothing serious. He's short of money again."

"Short of . . . I can't believe that kid! We paid all his MTC fees and left him plenty for haircuts and everything he'd need. He's been there six weeks and he's needed more money twice already. Wait'll your dad hears about this."

Later in the evening, after dinner, Jaci and Norm sat on the grass in the backyard. "What's with this kid?" Norm asked.

"I don't know," Jaci said. "He says he bought a few books, but he can't even take those with him, and the rest goes for snacks and things, I guess. Oh, and we know he sent Sherri flowers for her birthday."

"Yeah, he sends his girlfriend flowers with *our* money," Norm said with a shake of the head.

"As much as we've tried to teach our kids about saving money and being careful, I don't think Bart ever learned it," Jaci said.

"How could he *not* learn it? That's just the way we *do* things in our family," Norm protested.

"Oh, we *talked* about it plenty," Jaci said. "And I think our other kids learned pretty well. But you remember the disappointment Bart always felt when he didn't have money for things, don't you? We'd remind him he'd need to save for the future, and we assumed he'd learn better next time. But it was always the same. He never had money when he wanted it.

"I've decided now—a little late—that he never really knew how, never learned how, to save. He never actually figured out how to deny himself the things he wanted at the moment to save for the big things later."

If Jaci is right, Bart's "disappointment" was a message, a cry for help, unrecognized at the time by his parents. How easy it is to suppose that talking about, preaching, and exhorting are the same as teaching! "I don't know how any child of mine could *not* know how to save money," we say. "I've set a good example." But have we sat down and helped him set up a true system for saving—including a temptation-free hiding place or banking account?

We don't always remember that knowing the value of a concept isn't the same as knowing how to apply it. Many kids know they ought to save, yet they don't do it. (Of course kids aren't the only humans afflicted with the "I know better than I do" malady!)

We make a mistake when we imagine we've *taught* our kids to work hard, to save money, to help others, to think well—or any number of other things we value—when all we've done is *talk* about these ideas, however fervently and however often. People need to be shown *how* to apply the concepts to their lives.

What Does the Future Hold?

"But Dad," Reed moaned, as he flopped back on his bed, "studying is boring."

Dad had learned to know Reed's humor and knew his son was mostly trying to get a rise out of him. Nevertheless, Dad decided to use the occasion to pass on a few thoughts about schoolwork and the future.

"Oh, yes, it can be boring, all right," Dad said. "But so can digging ditches."

"Huh?"

"I want to be sure you're projecting consequences, son."

"Say what, Dad?"

Dad laughed and leaned on his elbow on Reed's study desk. "Oh, for all the years you've been in the family you've heard us talk about accepting the consequences of our decisions. That's what I'm talking about

—looking at what might happen if we do or don't do certain things."

"OK."

"You're in the ninth grade, so this year's grades don't really count on your high school GPA, as I understand it. But they set a pattern, and they're still important. Much of what you'll learn in the next three years will build on what you're doing now. Make sense?"

"Yep."

Dad was sure Reed wasn't very interested in the whole matter. He went on anyway. "So I think we ought to think through what will happen if your grades stay the same as they were last semester. Let's see, you had about a D— average, right?"

"What? I did not. I had a C or a C+."

Dad chuckled. "I know. I only wanted to see if you were listening."

"You should have seen what *some* people had."

"Yes, I'm sure. No one is saying a C is all that bad. After all, C is supposed to mean average. All I want us to do is to look at the consequences if that C gets projected right through your high school career. Let's say on graduation day you still have the C average. What now?"

"Well, I can still graduate, that's for sure," Reed said.

"Right. No problem there. What else?" Dad waited.

"Well . . . I could get a job."

"Yep, you could likely do that." Dad waited again.

"I might be able to go to college, some college," Reed said.

"Yes, you could get into certain schools. Not all poor ones, mind you. With open admission policies in many state schools, you could certainly get in. Of course, since certain college prep classes require more than a C in preceding work, that could get to be a problem.

"Since you've said for years you wanted to go to college, I assume getting into college is still important to you."

"Yes," Reed said.

"Of course, you've also said you wanted to go to one of two or three specific schools, none of which, I note, would likely accept a C average. You've also said you wanted to be a doctor. What about your C average then?"

"As long as I can get into college, won't I still be able to go on to medical school—assuming I do well in college?" Reed asked, obviously a little more interested by now.

"A good question," Dad said. "Let's talk about it. As I understand it . . ."

The message Dad has picked up from Reed is that not all of his son's study habits match his stated desires for future schooling. He's now helping Reed look ahead and see if the choices he makes today will bring the results he wants in the future.

Free agency is prized by all of us and certainly by teens. What they must be helped to realize is this: not only do consequences follow all of our choices, but we can often project how things will turn out if a present path is followed to the end. At some point things *do* matter, and it may be too late. This recognition is part of accepting responsibility.

Reed can, if he chooses, change his grade point average rather easily at this early stage. Whether he sees the matter as a problem worthy of his attention is mostly up to him. But it behooves his parents to help him see the connection between his present work and his future desires. Otherwise, his increasing independence will have been at least partly wasted.

5

Help Me Handle Conflicts and Disappointments

We all want our children to be successful in life. But even successful people encounter difficulties, disappointments, and failures. We may — sometimes unwisely — try to shield our children from many of these, but as hard as we try, this can't be done forever. Life will catch up with them. The question is how they will handle the problems life will bring them.

To one child, a poor performance on the basketball court means he's no good at sports. To another, it means he needs to put in more practice time on his dribbling and shooting so as to do better next time. One child interprets a poor report card as a sign she's dumb. Another decides to be more consistent with homework. The difference is that one has developed a "loser's limp," the other, a "winner's heart."

The difficulties our children encounter can either defeat them or teach them, depending on how they're handled. The child who decides to pick up and go on after a defeat is headed down a very different path than the one who decides his defeat makes him a failure. And parental attitudes will have a lot to say about which road a child will choose to take. On their own, children often have no idea how to interpret their difficulties; they don't have enough experience with life. That's where parents come in.

But before we can help our kids turn their particular mountains into molehills, we have to be keen observers. In the following vignettes, children send their parents and others around them specific messages about their difficulties and disappointments.

Show Me How to Handle Disappointment

Sam and Loni were enjoying the rare luxury of reading in bed, having managed to get there early for a change, when they heard somebody pounding up the stairs two at a time. Their son David burst into the room, his face white.

"Did you hear the news, Dad?" he exclaimed.

"No, what?" Sam asked in alarm. Loni put down her book.

"I was down watching the news," David said, a little breathlessly. "About Klemper and Elkington."

"Who?" Loni asked.

"You mean . . ." Sam started.

"Yeah," David said, "Harv Klemper and Chad Elkington, on the team."

Sam and Loni both knew that "the team" David referred to was the local university football team, whose play the family followed closely, with David being a near-fanatic fan. Klemper and Elkington were both first-string linebackers this year. "What about them?" Sam asked.

"They've been arrested for drugs," David said, his face showing disbelief.

As Sam analyzed his feelings later, he realized his first reaction to the news had actually been one of relief. David's tone had been so serious and distraught that Sam had feared he could be coming to report the assassination of the president or the outbreak of nuclear war somewhere. His relief faded quickly, however, watching the pain in his son's eyes as he related the details.

As Sam listened, he was sure he understood what David was going through. He'd been thirteen, only a year older than David was now, when he'd learned that one of his own idols, a country-western singer, was too drunk to make a scheduled appearance at a rodeo. The details weren't too clear now, but the memory of the pain was still vivid.

Sam and Loni are fortunate. Their son has come to them with his pain, rather than keeping it to himself or sharing it only with peers. Or, worst of all, not feeling it —out of a jaded outlook that "everybody does drugs these days."

As it is, David's horror is written all over his face, giving his parents a chance to help him work through the meaning of what he has just heard. Nothing they can say will likely rid him of the pain of disillusionment and disappointment. Nor is that necessary, since a certain number of such adjustments are part of growing up.

What his parents *can* do is to seize the opportunity to talk about the dangers of drugs, the need for vigilance and commitment in avoiding them, and the extreme power of peer pressure David will face in the next few years. This may be a teaching moment of the first order.

Of equal importance, Sam and Loni can discuss, tonight or at another time, the power of example. They can help David see the need to do the right thing in his future —partly for the reason that other impressionable young people will be watching him, just as he watched the team members who have now let him down.

How Do I Face Failure?

Cory Adams hunched on the mound like a hurt bird— knees up to hide his face—right under the bright sun, right in front of everyone, and bawled his eyes out. As soon as the last pitch had left his hand, he knew the throw was a terrible, irrevocable mistake. Instead of the sinker he had planned, the ball had escaped as nothing more than a plain old fast ball, and not a *very* fast one at that. It was straight and true, waist high and barely over the outside corner of the plate—the kind of pitch oversized Scat Watson loved more than chocolate ice cream.

In the instant of knowing the pitch wasn't right, Cory saw Scat start his swing and knew beyond any doubt that, short of a miracle the size of the Red Sea parting, the ball was gone, the game lost. But the sea stayed closed today and Cory's senses were filled immediately with the horror of having pitched to Scat Watson's third and most important home run of the playoff series.

In one slow-motion moment, such as people are said to feel as their car drives off a cliff or when they fall from a tall ladder, Cory noted the details of the tragedy before his eyes: the perfect swing, the high-pitched, metallic twang of aluminum on cowhide, the ball exploding over-head as if intent on leaving this globe on its exalted, climbing arc toward the empty pasture beyond the center field fence. Cory saw the teammates he had let down: in-fielders staring openmouthed, outfielders frozen in their places, mitts drooping at their sides, knowing there was no need to move.

In that same eternal instant, big Scat Watson started his unhurried jog toward first base, his arms high in the air, a laugh on his face, his body thrown upward in a twisting jump for joy. Cory heard the Red Sox stands erupt in a stupendous roar of ecstasy, while the silence from his own stunned Dodger boosters, whom he could not turn to face, beat down upon him in waves.

It is not too much to say that in this moment—to fourteen-year-old Cory Adams the most profound in history, the culminating instant in time toward which all previous centuries had pointed—he felt his very heart burst, his brain dissolve, his legs buckle, and the mound come up to meet him.

Why, oh, why did it have to end this way? Cory had not asked to pitch the bottom of the ninth inning of the final playoff game—a tied game in a tied series that would determine who went to state. Cory had never asked to face, of all batters, ominous Scat Watson, who was so big he had to carry a copy of his birth certificate to show the officials at every game that he qualified for the league age limits, and who had hit off of every Dodger pitcher in the series.

Cory had never wanted to pitch at all; outfield was his place. But Coach had seen his strong arm and had taught him a few useful pitches so he could fill in as needed on the mound. And sometimes he'd been pretty good. But why, oh, why, did he, a reluctant relief pitcher, have to be the one to lose the game, the series, the summer?

It wasn't fair, it wasn't right, it was an outrageous injustice. Cory suddenly hated the game he had for so long claimed to love more than life—this cruel, vicious game that took boys' hearts and mangled them like old, frayed baseballs. He never wanted to play, hear about, or think about baseball again. He simply wanted the mound to open up and swallow him before he had to face his dad in the stands, whose lips would say, "Son, it's only a game," but whose eyes would say, "Couldn't you throw just one more sinker? You know how Scat hates sinkers."

Ah, how poignantly life's crucial moments are often perceived. Sometime soon Cory will realize the world didn't really stop turning, that he alone did not lose the game and the series, and that it's "only a game," after all. But for the moment, there is nothing like the abject misery of being the center of attention—as both pitchers and batters tend to be in the "all-American pastime"—and failing, right before the eyes of foes, whom we want to put in their place, and of friends, whose trust we want to continue to merit.

Of course, baseball *is* a cruel game. It does sometimes put too much pressure on individuals. But maybe that's one of the reasons why it's the all-American favorite—because it resembles *life*, which also sometimes puts the same pressures on individuals.

What we learn as we grow up is that we will sometimes succeed and sometimes fail. Furthermore, we learn the difficult lesson that either one is acceptable if we have done our best. If Cory doesn't learn it at fourteen, he will have to learn it at twenty-four or forty-four or sixty-four, because everyone fails at times.

If Cory's dad is sensitive, he will realize that Cory could use a boost right now. And if he's careful, he will make sure Cory knows through subsequent discussions and comments that failure has less to do with facts than with state of mind.

Unfortunately, no one remembers the other bad pitches thrown in this and earlier games by various pitchers on both teams, when the last pitch "loses" the game. That's one of the troubles with baseball, and with life: Certain things get weighted all out of proportion to their value.

But Cory can be helped to accept the fact that life is like that. He will always be facing, in one form or other, the Scat Watsons of life. And on some days, his best won't be enough. Sometimes old Scat will swagger up to the plate and take a bite out of the moon with the ball, no matter how well it's pitched. But other times, his first, second, and third swings will make only hollow swishes through the still air, and even the great Scat will have to take his turn at a slow walk back to the dugout.

Parents who help their children obtain sufficient success experiences must also be sure to help them accept that there will be days when they fail. We must teach them that *failure* isn't a bad word. And when we say so, we must be sure our eyes match our lips.

Show Me How to Seek Solutions

It's nearly 10:00 P.M. and Liz is at the kitchen counter, loading the dishwasher while she cradles the phone on her shoulder. Suddenly her fifth-grader, Shelley, is at her side, in tears.

"Just a minute, Mother," Liz says into the phone. Then, "What's the matter, Shelley? I thought you were in bed."

"I was," Shelley says, "but I left my homework at school. I just remembered."

Let's stop here for a moment. Liz is faced with a choice. Confronted with the interruption of a pleasant long-distance conversation with her mother, her inclination is to tell Shelley it's too late to do anything about forgotten homework now and to get back in bed. But let's see what she does.

"Shelley, why don't you sit down for a minute while I finish talking to Grandma, and I'll talk with you about it."

Shelley pulls out a kitchen chair from the table and sits. Liz hopes the delay will give her high-strung daughter time to calm down. To help her do so, she wipes her hands on a towel and stands behind her with a hand on her shoulder. By the time she finishes talking with her mother, her daughter is settled down pretty well.

It turns out there's not much to tell. Shelley has a math assignment due first thing tomorrow and she simply forgot to bring home the mimeographed sheet of work.

At this point, Liz faces another choice. Since the same thing has happened a few other times this year, Liz has to decide whether to "teach" her daughter a lesson about thinking ahead and being conscientious. In this case, she feels Shelley is upset enough already—which, in itself, indicates conscientiousness—without a parental dose of musts and shoulds.

"Tell you what," Liz says. "Since there's nothing we can do about it tonight, why don't you get up a few minutes early and get ready really fast, and I'll run you over to school by 8:20. Isn't that when the doors open? Will that give you time to get done before the bell?"

Shelley's message is one of sorrow and anxiety, presenting her mother with numerous options. And Liz seems to have handled her choices well. By offering solutions, she is helping her daughter learn to respond rationally as well as emotionally to life's inevitable difficulties.

Sometimes, children probably need the "you-made-the-mistake-so-you'll-have-to-live-with-the-consequences" speech, particularly when patterns develop and parental bailout becomes an expectation. But there are also situations where comfort and solutions are needed.

Tonight, Shelley can sleep well for two reasons: first, because her homework will get done on time, and second, because her mother supplied not only sympathy but also a solution.

Help Me Avoid Childhood Burnout

It was Alice's turn, and she stepped up to the desk. "Mrs. Carlton, I'm Alice Renquist. Rebecca's mother."

"Oh, certainly. Sit down, please. I'm sorry you had to wait so long in line, but it's hard to keep to five-minute interviews at parent-teacher conferences. At least, *I* have trouble with that."

oblem. How's Becky doing?"

ire her scores on the sixth-grade national tests

y finished. They're good, and we can look at those in more detail if you'd like. And in her class work, Becky is doing fine." Mrs. Carlton paused.

"Yes? Is anything wrong?" Alice asked.

"Well, I hesitate to say anything, but I've wondered if she isn't slipping a little lately. I don't mean to alarm you. Her work is still good, and maybe it's only a stage. But the last few weeks, it does seem as if she's a bit distracted —not as able to concentrate and get down to work."

"She's been that way at home, too," Alice said. "We've noticed it. She's always been so conscientious about things, but lately she has been kind of listless."

"Yes, that's the word I was looking for. There might, of course, be a physical problem. You may want to have her checked. It may also be simply a matter of maturation and the onset of adolescence. But I've also seen kids who get kind of—well, burned out, mentally or emotionally. They try to do so many things, and they're so busy all the time, that they're under a lot of stress. They sometimes come to a point where they kind of fade a little. They can't keep up with it all."

The message Becky is sending her parents and teacher may be critical. It could be a call for help. Some kids in our society are as over-programmed and driven as are many adults. This may lead them to drugs or depression in early adolescence. Pediatricians have even discovered four-year-olds with peptic ulcers.

It behooves parents to examine whether their children exhibit characteristics of malaise or stress. Abrupt behavior changes like Becky's are symptoms needing examination.

While we want our kids to learn responsibility, we want them also to enjoy their childhood. Often this means less structure and more time to relax.

The world pulls from many directions, and one of the essential questions we need to help our children with is "What really matters?" With such perspective, burnout (at any age) need not occur.

Help Me Learn to Express Concern

"Mommie, where are you?"

"Right here, honey. In the yard, weeding."

Aaron came down the driveway and around the corner of the house. "Mom," he said, "I have a concern."

This phrase coming from three-year-old Aaron's puckered little mouth nearly made his mother laugh out loud. He sounded so grown-up and his face looked so serious! She pulled Aaron down on the warm grass beside her and listened to his concern — over the sharing of a toy truck with his playmate from next door — and sent him on his way feeling better. Then she sat back to think about her young son's use of the statement that had changed their family for the better.

Only a short time ago, Aaron's response would have been to grab the toy he wanted and run. Now, he tried to talk about it.

The "I have a concern" phrase had come first from Sarah, who brought it home from the fifth grade a few weeks ago. "That's what we're supposed to say when we're upset or want to settle a problem with someone," Sarah had explained in a family home evening lesson she had requested to teach. "Instead of hitting or slamming doors or crying or something, you say to the person, 'I have a concern,' and then you say what you feel. Together you solve the problem."

It had sounded too simple to Sarah's parents, although they honored her request to try it. And they had been pleasantly surprised at how useful the approach was. Now, even Aaron had picked up the phrase to express his frustrations.

Sarah and Aaron's parents are wise to have supported Sarah's efforts at stating feelings and concerns in honest ways. While no statement or series of statements will resolve all frustrations in family encounters, an attitude of talking rather than fighting will go a long way toward solving problems. Sarah and Aaron are fortunate to grow up in a home where they are encouraged to state how they feel and where parents will listen to those concerns.

And interestingly, the simplest, most open and honest approaches usually work best. When we apply them regularly and teach our children to do so, we can create a family where people learn how to handle difficulties rather than run from them.

Is Life Fair?

The family waited expectantly before the TV set. "Are you sure Tim's on tonight, Mom?"

"Yes, I'm sure. His mom told me herself. She said it would be on the local news on channel eight."

"Here it comes," Dad said.

"There he is!" one of the children said.

"Shhh. Listen," another said.

Tim Morley, young friend and neighbor of the Mc-Cormick family's for all the years they'd lived on Forsythia Drive, appeared on the screen. How unnatural to see him on TV instead of eating popcorn in their kitchen or skiing with the family or playing basketball in the driveway. But how much more unnatural to see him for the first time in a wheelchair, a paraplegic.

Tim was being interviewed by a local news team from a clinic in another state where he had been since his accident.

"He's lost a lot of weight," John said, as if to himself. John was Tim's age and one of his best friends. No one answered, but John's comment reminded Mom of the time, right after the accident, when John had asked her, "Why, Mom? Why Tim? He was such a good person."

"He still *is* a good person, John," she had said.

"I know," John said, "but I mean he wasn't doing anything wrong, so it's not like he needed to be punished or something. He was just driving along and an idiot drunk comes along and smashes him. It's not fair."

Tears came to her eyes as Mom remembered this and other conversations she and her husband had had with John, where they could only say, "You're right, John. It's not fair. It's terrible, it's rotten. And of course Tim wasn't being purposely punished. Still, it happened. We can only go on."

As Tim spoke to the interviewer, it became clear he'd had similar questions. He said, "You know, when I first woke up here, I kept asking myself, 'Why?' I couldn't accept it. I'd played sports in high school, thinking of a career in baseball. And then this? And I couldn't believe it was really me lying here not even able to move—not even one toe.

"But something happened. Two things, really. When I got so I could sit in a wheelchair, I started to get around the ward a little. And I saw things. I saw people who were a lot worse off than I was. I saw people who not only couldn't walk, they couldn't even move out of bed. I saw people who couldn't talk. I saw lots and lots of quadriplegics. And I didn't even know what the word meant before I came here, I'm ashamed to admit. But here were people who couldn't move any limb at all. I can use my arms and hands just great. And I started to realize I could have been a lot worse off, a lot.

"And then another thing happened. I got a special letter. You know, I'd received a lot of letters since I'd been here, and cards, from friends at school and home. And I should thank them right here because I'm a lousy letter writer. I'll never get around to answering most of them."

Tim and the interviewer both laughed and the interviewer said, "Now's your chance. Go ahead."

"I do appreciate all of those," Tim said, looking into the camera. "But there was one letter, from a very special friend. His name is John McCormick."

"That's you!" screamed Maria, the youngest. "That's my brother," she said to the TV. John looked at his parents, who were as surprised as he was.

Tim went on. "See, John is my best friend at home. And he wrote me a letter about two months ago. I did write him back—he's one of the few—but I never really told him what his letter meant to me. Can I read part of it? It might help somebody else."

"Sure," the interviewer said.

Tim read:

> Tim, when the accident happened to you, I couldn't believe it. I lay awake asking myself why and how a thing like this could happen. People

kept telling me it was God's will and everything was under control. They're probably right, but it didn't help me understand. I wasn't doubting God; I was only trying to figure it all out, and I couldn't.

Well, once when I was talking to my folks about it, my mom said something that really had an effect on me. I didn't like it at first, because it didn't sound like a real answer, just sort of a way around it. But the more I thought about it, the more clear it became that it really is the answer, or part of one. I'm going to tell you what she said and hope the idea will help you, too.

She said, "John, life really isn't fair. It was never promised to be fair. The scriptures don't even come close to promising fairness in this life. But they do say God knows everything that happens and they also say good will prevail in the end."

"So what does that prove?" I asked her. "How does it explain Tim's problem?"

"Well," she said, "if life isn't fair, you can quit wasting your energy worrying about it! You can turn your life over to God and let him work with you however he can. You can find your own purpose."

Tim, I don't know what all this means to you, but to me it means to make the most of anything. Good can come of this thing, and life is still worth living. But you have to find your own purpose. I guess we all do. It's only been forced on you quicker than on some of the rest of us.

Tim looked back at the camera. "There's more," he said, "but that's the main idea. So, if John is back home watching, I want to tell him—and his mom—he might have saved my life with that letter. What a simple idea

—that life isn't meant to be fair—but it helped me get over worrying about the wrong thing. I don't know if I've found my purpose yet, but I'm working on it. It's still hard but I'm not bitter anymore."

There are stages of life in which fairness seems paramount, or—turned around—where *un*fairness is a major and intolerable preoccupation. And where there is unfairness, in the home in sibling relations and in other matters that can be cleared up, doing so should be a parental priority.

But on another level, when our children send us a message about the unfairness of the bigger things in life, we can help them adjust to the idea that they will not always find equity and fairness. Some who appear to deserve a great deal in terms of this world's comforts obtain very few. Others who seem to disdain everything we call good manage to live in high style and with apparent ease and comfort. It isn't fair!

The best message a parent can sometimes give a child is: 'That's right. It isn't fair. Things will all work out in the eternities. But for now, for your own life, don't waste your energy worrying. Get on with your life."

6

Help Me Give of Myself

"I'd be glad to, Mother!" What parent (perhaps after being revived!) wouldn't be thrilled at such a statement of helpfulness and desire to give? How much more often most of us probably hear "Why me?" "I already did my share," "It's not fair," or "It's *mine.*"

If the home is truly a laboratory in which to practice the values of living, what better value is there than the desire to serve and help others? Children, we're told, go through selfish stages in which they think only of themselves, as well as "giving" stages when they feel joy in helping others. It's obvious which of these is preferable to parents, but there's no guarantee that the spirit of giving will automatically win out.

Wise parents will do more than model service and a spirit of giving. They will also openly encourage, reward, and promote such attitudes. This can be done only when they keep their eyes and ears open for positive experiences to support or negative ones to correct. Some of each are seen in the following stories.

Help Me Cultivate Consideration

Phil parked the car in the driveway and headed for the front door. After a busy day at work, he had momentarily forgotten what day it was until he passed the jack-o'-lanterns on the front step, their hand-carved, lop-sided grins looking more silly than sinister. Phil stepped into an entryway hung with fake cobwebs, huge crepe spiders, and dancing paper skeletons.

"Boo!" a voice yelled. Ten-year-old Meg was waiting behind the door. "Trick-or-treat!"

"Boo, yourself," Phil said, as he gave her a hug.

"Dad," she said, "I need to talk to you." She suddenly seemed kind of serious.

"What's the matter, honey?"

"Oh, nothing's wrong," she smiled, "but I need to ask you something."

Phil could tell from the look on her face that this wasn't likely a terribly serious matter. Yet she did look concerned and a little reticent.

"OK, what is it?" Phil asked.

"It can wait a minute. You go ahead and take your coat off and things," Meg directed. "I'll be in my room."

As Phil went down the hall, he marvelled at how grown up Meg was becoming, and he wondered suspiciously if he was being conned into something. He greeted his wife and asked her if she knew what Meg was concerned about.

"No clue," Pat said. "She's been bustling around here getting ready for trick-or-treating, talking about what she's going to wear for a costume and things. She seemed fine."

"She kind of has a 'cat-ate-the-canary' look," Phil said. "I wonder what she wants." In the bedroom, he changed clothes before going to Meg's room. In a few minutes he came out and went to the kitchen to talk to Pat again.

"Well, guess what," he began quietly.

"What did she want?" Pat asked.

"I had it wrong. I misinterpreted as coyness what turned out to be merely a concern for me. Do you know what the little darling wanted? She started off like this, 'Dad, you know how you always go around with us trick-or-treating on Halloween?'

" 'Yes,' I said.

" 'Well,' she said, 'Malin and Jody asked if I could go with them tonight — just in the neighborhood, like we always do. I told them I'd have to see, because I didn't want you to feel bad. I'll go with you and the little kids if you want me to.' Amazing, isn't she?"

Here is a child who is communicating a message any parent would be thrilled to hear: concern for others, even in the so-called little things. Meg is the type who will likely please her parents in future years by seriously considering their feelings about her decisions.

Whether Pat and Phil have consciously cultivated this trait in their daughter or she is "just that way," the result is the same. But they can help ensure that she stays that way. Besides modeling considerate behavior, parents can praise it when they see it. A note from Phil about how pleased he was with her kindness, waiting on Meg's pillow when she returns from trick-or-treating, will be a great reinforcer.

How easy to call attention only to the selfish behavior our children display, letting the good things slide by as if they're merely expected! We call attention to the wrong things, then wonder why our kids aren't as helpful, considerate, or thoughtful as they used to be.

I Want to Help, but of My Own Free Will

"What was that all about?" Jean asked after listening from another room as her husband had words with their son.

Mac was angry. "That was a case of a sixteen-year-old smart-mouth arguing with his dad."

"Terry's usually pretty careful, isn't he?" Jean asked.

"Actually, compared to some kids, he wasn't all *that* mouthy, I guess." Mac was calming down now. "All he really said was 'No, thanks, I guess not.'"

"Oh?" Jean said. "You'd better tell me more than that!"

Mac sat down. "Well," he said, "maybe I caused it. That's why I didn't chase him down when he went to his room. You know what a poor job he did of substituting on Cally's paper route this afternoon. Well, when she told me her bike tire won't hold air again, I told him he could fix it. That's when he said 'No thanks.'"

"Why, I thought he liked fixing flats. He's done them all for years."

"Yep. But the rest of the story," Mac added sheepishly, "is that I actually said, 'Since you did such a sloppy job on Cally's route, you can fix her tire for her.'"

Ah ha! The truth will out. Mac's honesty indicates he understands already what went wrong. Simply put, what his son Terry used to do for fun suddenly sounds like a punishment. If Mac will now follow up his honest discussion with his wife by an honest visit with his boy, he has a good chance to fix things up without leaving Terry with a permanent distaste for patching bike tires — or for helping in other ways.

How easily we can turn a free-will offering from enjoyment into punishment! In the future, if Terry needs disciplining because of his poor work, his parents will likely try to find more appropriate means than robbing him of an enjoyable service experience.

Learning to Share

The hot June sun beat down on the highway and made Sid conscious of his gratitude for the inventor of automobile air conditioning. He turned into the driveway from work just as a delivery truck pulled away from the curb. "Who got the package, honey?" was the first question for his wife when he came in the house.

"It was another one for Kirk," Melba said. "He acted like he didn't want me to see it, and he hurried right to his room with it. It was big and looked heavy."

"That kid," Sid said impatiently. "When's he going to stop ordering all these things from his catalogs and settle down to really saving? He needs to get money together for a mission, and he's only got another six months or so to do it. I wish he could get serious."

"Oh, he's not doing too badly, Sid," Melba said. "He's saving a lot better than he did. And having any real money is kind of new to him. But you're right — all these tapes and hunting shirts and things he orders, he could certainly get along without right now. This box was bigger than any of those usual things. I don't know what it could be."

"Did he say anything? Did you ask him about it?"

"He saw me watching as he signed for it. And he gave me a look that said, 'Never mind, Mom.' I got the message."

"Well," Sid said, "I'm going down and see what he's done."

"Sid," Melba said, "another thing. I'm hesitant to mention it, but the package was COD, and I heard the man ask for a hundred and some dollars."

"Good night!" Sid exclaimed. "He's really done it this time." Sid turned and went down the stairs two at a time. He knocked on Kirk's bedroom door, loudly, to be heard over the stereo.

"Hi, Dad," Kirk said when he opened the door.

Sid turned down the volume before he answered. "Hi, son," he said. He looked around the room. There was no package in sight. "Mom says you got another package today."

"Yeah," Kirk said noncommittally.

"An expensive one, it seems," Sid added. When Kirk didn't answer, Sid went on. "Kirk," he said, "you know how we feel about this. Now that you're working full-time these last few months before your mission . . ."

"Dad," Kirk interrupted, "it's Mom's birthday present. That's all. Want to see? I hid it in my closet."

Five minutes later Sid paused at the foot of the stairs before going back up to Melba, and shook his head in amazement. Slowly, he started up. How much more subdued he felt now, compared to how he'd felt when he'd come down these same steps a few minutes before.

Melba sat on the top step, looking at the evening

paper she'd brought in off the porch a moment before. "Well?" she said.

"Melba," Sid said, "that's quite a boy you have there." To her questioning look, he added, "And you're going to have to wait a few days to know what's in that package."

Sid went out of the back door to turn on the back sprinklers, but mostly to avoid Melba's questions. As he stood and watched the cool spray fall on the thirsty grass, he marvelled at the story he'd just heard.

Kirk had seen an ad for a mail order sewing machine. It had appeared to him to have all the features his mom's twenty-year-old machine lacked. The ad assured him the machine—for only $119.99 plus shipping—had the "quality, guarantee, and capabilities of machines costing up to $500 or more!" And, sure enough, he'd ordered one for his mom's birthday.

Sid was astounded. Sure, Kirk was earning comparatively "big" money now, but he'd probably never spent more than five dollars on his mom's birthday before, and sometimes quite a bit less. Sid was also worried. The machine in the box was heavy and old-fashioned looking, a very basic model. It looked adequate, but he was certain Melba would prefer her trusty, lightweight Elna, in spite of its age. Maybe he'd have to give her advance warning. But somehow, he knew they'd work it out.

Sid is experiencing one of the glowing moments of parenthood. He may still wish his son would save his money better, but somehow financial matters don't seem very important at the moment. Right now, it's enough to see his son's budding generosity and joy in giving. It's a fine message for a child to send. Fortunately, Sid "got" the message, and recognized what this particular expenditure on his son's part was really all about. Dad made a wise choice not to turn the discussion of the purchase into a lesson on wise consumerism.

This is a birthday Melba will never forget. Kirk may yet have more to learn about mail order advertising claims, but there's nothing wrong with his heart, and that's the best present a mother could have.

Sibling Rivalry

Dan was on his way out of the door when he saw his oldest daughter's light on in her room. He knocked on the door and said, "Come on, Sandy, everybody else is in the car."

Sandy opened the door. "Sandy!" Dan said. "You're still in your jeans. You'll make us late."

"I'm not going, Dad. Didn't Mom tell you?"

"No, she didn't. Not going?" Dan said with surprise. "Why on earth not? This is Johnnie's big night."

"I'm sick of violin music," Sandy said shortly.

"Sandy," Dan said. "We're not talking about violin music here. We're talking about Johnnie's performance award."

"I know," Sandy said. "I guess I've heard about enough of Johnnie and his violin awards." She turned away.

Dan stared at his daughter in exasperation, then pulled the door shut, probably harder than normal. "I don't have time to argue," he thought, as he joined the rest of the family for the drive to the auditorium.

Later that night, after the ceremonies at which fifteen-year-old Johnnie received a state "Young Talent" award, Dan and his wife Noreen were getting ready for bed. "What's with Sandy?" Dan asked. "I can't believe she wouldn't come tonight."

"I could tell by the way she was talking this afternoon that she probably wasn't coming," Noreen said.

"Why didn't you tell her she had to?"

"For one thing," Noreen said, "she's seventeen years old. We haven't been in the habit of telling her very often anymore what she *has* to do."

"Well, I don't mean she 'had to,' but didn't you tell her it was an important thing for the family?"

"Yes, I did," Noreen said, "but I sensed she was making some kind of statement and wasn't about to be budged. I was going to mention it to you, but then when you had car trouble and got home late, everything was so hectic, I forgot to say anything about it."

"I still can't believe it. What does she mean, she's heard enough about Johnnie and his violin awards?"

"Well, the main reason I didn't push it today is that I remember the ugly incident last month when we gave Johnnie the new camera for his tour with the youth symphony."

"Oh, yes, that was lovely, all right," Dan said. "You'd have thought Noreen was four instead of nearly eighteen. 'Why Johnnie? Why does he get a new camera and mine hasn't worked right for years?' I can hear it now."

"Yes, and all the reasoning in the world about Johnnie needing one for the trip and about it really being just an early birthday present made no impression," Noreen said. "I think she felt a little ashamed of herself later, but

I don't think she changed her mind about being some-what cheated."

Dan nodded.

"So," Noreen went on, "I think I see a pattern here we need to address. I'm surprised I didn't see it before."

If Sandy's parents would be able to get her to honestly answer the question of who her parents' favorite child is, what would her answer be? Most children feel that there is a favorite child in their family. They may think it is themselves or they may feel it is someone else in the family, but they tend to think *someone* is the favorite.

Parents almost always deny having favorites, saying they love each child equally and treat them the same. The paranoia of youth, however, doesn't always let our efforts at fairness come through.

Apparently Sandy is experiencing difficulty with the attention her younger brother is receiving. While this might be a surprising message, it's an important one, no matter at what age it appears.

The problem won't go away by telling Sandy not to be silly. But Dan and Noreen will be wise to analyze their behavior and make sure they haven't come across as elevating Johnnie over their other children through the attention his musical ability receives. They will also be wise to help Sandy look at her own attitudes and learn to accept that her parents can be proud of her brother's accomplishments without rejecting her in any way.

Sibling Love

"Oh, I can't do this!" Heather exclaimed, jumping up from the dining room table where she had her homework spread out, and going to the kitchen for a drink of water.

"What's the prob, kid?" Heather's older sister Cheryl asked, looking up from loading the dishwasher. "Seventh grade too tough for you?"

"Yes!" Heather said. "I quit."

"Well, I'm afraid they don't allow that. At least they didn't when I was there. What are you working on?"

"Math. Pre-algebra. I hate it."

"I did too," Cheryl said. She dried her hands and followed Heather back to the table. "Let me see it."

"I don't get it at all," Heather said. "How can you mix numbers and letters together anyway?"

"Well, I'm not sure I really understand that *yet*, but I do know how to do it," Cheryl said. "It's sort of like a game, when you see what you're supposed to do. Want me to help? Or do you want to suffer alone?"

Heather grinned. "I'll take any help that can make sense out of this stuff."

A few minutes later Heather was able to work out each problem she came to. "Thanks," she said to her sister.

"It took me a while to understand that the main thing is to keep up each day, and to ask questions as soon as you're not sure. It'll make sense in time." Cheryl shook her head. "Listen to me. I sound like a parent."

The parents of these two should count themselves blessed to see an attitude of helpfulness and giving between them—particularly a few minutes later, when Heather is seen helping Jon with his third-grade social studies work sheet. Attitudes do get passed down, good ones as well as bad ones.

Children who live in a home where helpfulness and giving to others extends even to their own siblings (sometimes the hardest people to help or show friendship to) will develop deep and lifelong family friendships.

Sibling rivalry is common enough to be called natural. But expressions of sibling love occur too, and must be cultivated and praised. If they occur less frequently than hoped, their very rarity should cause us to notice and remark upon them.

Showing Sensitivity

"Man, what a day," Glen thought, as he sat beside the tow truck driver who was pulling the station wagon into the shop. "First, the late start this morning, then the near miss in that three-car pileup, then the stupid car breaking down just as we were nearly to our motel — not to mention the kids fighting all day in the car. What a vacation!

"Now, here we are stranded, for who knows how many days, in a little town two states away from home, while they try to figure out what's wrong and whether they have the parts. At least the station is only three blocks from the motel, so we can keep our eye on things."

A few minutes later, as Glen waited impatiently beside his vehicle for the night mechanic to have a chance to look at it, he was startled to see Shawn, his sixteen-year-old—the main cause of most of today's contention in the car—coming down the sidewalk. The sight of him renewed Glen's frustration. He couldn't believe how much teasing, whining, and complaining four kids could cause on a trip. And this was only the second day out.

He was particularly upset with Shawn, who, in spite of being the oldest, had acted like a selfish brat for most of today, complaining constantly that it was taking too long to get to the beach and the amusement parks they planned to visit. Next year, he hoped, Shawn would decide to stay home from the family's summer trip. There came an age when a kid was just too much trouble to drag along.

"What do they think, Dad?" Shawn asked.

"Nobody's even looked yet," Glen said.

"Here's a sandwich," Shawn said. "Mom made 'em. She says we can't eat out tonight, because we need to save money in case the car is expensive to fix."

Glen looked at the sandwich with a total lack of interest. "Put it in the car." It had been a long time since lunch, but Glen never could eat when he was upset, and right now his stomach was practicing tying itself in knots. And to think that all day he'd looked forward to a hot meal tonight. Had *anything* gone right today?

Glen was deciding to tear into Shawn for his immature behavior today when the mechanic came to check the car. With his head under the hood, he asked several questions, had Glen try to start the engine, and made a few simple tests. "Tell you what," he said, "I'm going to call my boss, the day man. He knows a lot more about these older 350s than I do. Maybe he'll come down and have a look. We're open all night, so if he can get me started right, and if we have the parts, we might have this thing going for you by morning."

"Man, that would be great!" Glen said. He tried not to get his hopes up yet, but he was feeling a lot better already.

The mechanic stepped into the office to phone, and Shawn said, "Dad?"

"Huh?" Shawn looked serious. In a flash, Glen had an image of Shawn apologizing for today's misdemeanors. Wouldn't that be something? "No," he thought, "that would be too much to expect."

Shawn went on. "If we don't get out of here for a while, Mom's already asking people what there is to do around here. There's a pool at the motel that the little kids are probably already in, and there's a small pioneer museum up the street. There's a park down by the river, and there's probably other stuff around."

Glen was surprised. "What about Magic Mountain? I thought we couldn't get there fast enough for you?"

Shawn shrugged. "We're here now, so we'd just as well make the most of it. I told the other kids not to make trouble, since there's nothing we can do to change things. It's kind of fun, Dad, kind of an adventure — as long as it doesn't cost too much to fix this old crate."

Glen was amazed at Shawn's attitude. Maybe this was sort of an apology, after all.

Just then the mechanic called out from the office, "The boss is on his way. Who knows what he'll find, but he will find it. He's good — and he's honest."

"Thanks a lot," Glen answered. He put his hand on Shawn's shoulder. "And thank you, son, for coming over. Now, where'd you put that sandwich? I'm starved."

Glen realizes he's expecting too much for his sixteen-year-old son to apologize outright for being less than helpful in the car today. But in an indirect way, apologizing is really what he's doing by his mature, sensitive approach, isn't it?

As the oldest child in the family, Shawn has come through when he's needed. His acceptance of the inevitable, his leadership of his siblings, and his tacit admission that he was part of today's problem, all have contributed to helping out his dad. What parent could ask for more?

And while Shawn's behavior on the next hard day on the road may again be back to "normal," and less than perfect, he has nevertheless been a great comfort to his dad tonight, sending a sweet message of giving of himself.

Parents who notice and praise such behavior will find it increasing, and in so doing they reap one of the greatest rewards of parenthood.

7

Help Me Feel Loved and Appreciated

One of the ironies of parenthood is how a parent can give so much time and effort to the task and yet raise children who feel unloved. "Not loved?" a parent exclaims. "Everything I did, I did for my family."

"But we didn't *feel* you cared about us," comes the bitter reply. "So what if you fed us and clothed us? That just seemed to be your duty. You never acted like you had time for us or a real interest in what we were doing." These would be sad words, indeed.

A study made in 1988 asked parents whether they felt their children would confide in them if they were involved in drug abuse. Fifty percent of the parents said they thought so. The same question asked of youth brought a different response: seventy percent said they'd go to a friend, eight percent would go to a sibling, and only twenty percent would go to their parents. The level of trust isn't as high as parents hope.

If parents don't give conscious effort to showing their children they are loved, appreciated, listened to, and trusted, they probably won't get the message. Loving our kids isn't enough; they have to somehow *know* we do. Otherwise, the messages they send back will communicate their feeling of rejection, as shown in some of the following vignettes.

I Need to Feel Appreciated

"What weather!" Allen said quietly.

"It's great, isn't it?" Arnold answered. "I've never seen it so warm in deer season."

The two friends sat on a ridge in the early dawn, waiting for a buck to appear. They'd hunted these same canyons every fall for years. Whether or not they brought home a deer, the tradition was important.

Over the next few minutes, while they waited and watched, the two men talked, and the conversation moved from previous hunts to careers.

Arnold asked, "I've never asked you, but I've always been curious how you got into cooking before you started trucking."

"Oh, I started in a hamburger place when I was in high school and I got a little experience with it. So when I graduated, the easiest thing to do seemed to be to apply as a cook. I started as a night cook at a truck stop. I stayed there about two years, moved up to days. Could have stayed with it, I guess, 'cause I enjoyed it and did well at it, but I got the offer to drive for Midway Lines, and I left cooking behind. I'd even thought about going to a cooking school and making a career of it."

"I thought maybe you'd cooked at home, as a kid."

"No," Allen said. "On the farm, in those days, we boys didn't do many indoor chores. The only time I remember cooking was once when I was about eleven. My little sister and I decided to make Mom a cake for Mother's Day. Dad got Mom away someplace and we went to work—from scratch, mind you.

"It came out OK, but the part I remember is not knowing what the book meant by 'cream the shortening.' I took some cream off the milk in the fridge and stirred it in!" He laughed and went on. "I guess the stirring got enough lumps out of the shortening, and the cream probably actually helped the recipe, because it came out OK."

Both men laughed. No more was said as they scanned the hills in the increasing light.

"Actually," Allen said, "there was one other experience with cooking at home, a negative one. I haven't thought of it in years, but I guess it's still a little painful."

"Oh?" Arnold said. He waited.

"Well, I was thirteen, I think, and my mom was sick for a few days, right down in bed. That was pretty unusual for her, so we knew she was really sick. One night, my sister and I decided we'd fix dinner. She was too little to do it alone, and Dad was busy, and—anyway, we did it. I remember we did macaroni and cheese.

"I don't remember the details; but I know Mom kind of got after us for the mess we made and for using too much cheese and what-all. We made enough to feed us for a week, I think. Macaroni swells up, you know."

Allen smiled slightly. "I wonder why I remember that part so well, about Mom being upset. I knew she was sick, so maybe she was grouchy, and I couldn't hold that against her 'cause she didn't feel good. But it did bother me. I guess I felt like I was doing a great thing and she didn't appreciate it, or something. Silly.

"I remember thinking how a neighbor had brought in supper the night before, and Mom didn't complain at all about that meal, even though it wasn't the kind of food we ate. In fact, she wrote a nice thank-you note."

"Silly," Allen says, that he should remember needing to feel appreciated. He feels ashamed of what seems petty now. But the memory remains. People, including children, need appreciation, and that isn't silly.

Allen's mother missed recognizing a need in her child. Perhaps she was out of sorts because of her illness. But perhaps, too, her timing was off quite a lot. As a conscientious mother, she wanted to teach her children to clean up their messes, to conserve resources, and to avoid waste—all valuable lessons. But in emphasizing these points, she apparently omitted conveying gratitude for efforts made on her behalf, thereby leaving her son— who felt he'd gone out of his way—feeling unappreciated.

Children will forgive their parents for such omissions, especially as they recognize a few of their own, but the effect can remain in feelings of rejection. How much better to grow up feeling appreciated.

Please Like Me

The back door opened. "Mom?" Talia called.

"I'm in here, honey," Mom answered. When her daughter came into the bedroom, Mom added, "Thanks for coming home so fast when I called you."

"You're welcome," Talia said. "I was tired of playing at Lynne's anyway."

"Oh? Well, you're learning to come quickly, and that's good."

" 'Cause I'm big now, huh? I'm five."

"That's right. You're big."

"Mom?"

"Yes."

"You like me, huh?"

"Like you! Why, of course I like you! I love you to bits!" Mom said, as she grabbed her daughter and pretended to gobble her up. They fell on the bed. Talia giggled.

"But, Mom, even when I'm mean or naughty, huh?" she asked.

"What?"

"You like me, even when I'm naughty?" Talia was very serious.

"Why, of course I do. I always like you, even when I don't like what you're doing at the time. I've told you that. Why, honey?"

"Well, at Lynne's, she was mad at her mom 'cause she wouldn't let us take the dolls outside. Lynne said, 'I don't like you,' and her mom said, 'Well, I don't like you either.' You wouldn't say that, would you, Mom?"

Talia is giving her mother a chance to reinforce a child's need for unconditional love. Lynne's mother failed the test.

While our children may not ever ask us flat out if we "like" them or love them, as Talia did, they will always want to know. And while most of us won't make the mistake Lynne's mother made by making an immature response to a childish statement, we may make another mistake: We may assume our children know our love is constant and unwavering and that it doesn't depend on their behavior.

Unless we tell them, repeatedly and sincerely, how will they know?

Help Me When I Need It

"Mom, come quick," Kelly called from the front stairs.

"What is it?" Mom asked.

"It's a thing. I can't remember its name. On the front railing."

"A thing, huh?" Mom set the hand mixer on the counter and followed her excited eight-year-old daughter out of the front door.

"Don't scare it," Kelly said. "See, right there. It's like a big green grasshopper."

"Oh, that. That's a katydid, I think." Mom backed away slightly.

"Yeah, that's it. We learned about them in school. Look how he just sits there. You can't even tell if he's alive."

"Well, he's alive, all right. That's why I'm not getting any closer. I'm not an insect fan." Mom started back into the house.

"They sing at night, or rub their legs like crickets. Can I catch him?"

"Maybe you can," Mom said. "I have to finish dinner."

"But, Mom," Kelly said, "how? How can we catch him?"

"Not *we*, Kelly, *you*," Mom said. "I told you I'm not a fan of six-legged creatures."

"Me neither, except when they're in jars. But I want to take him to school."

"That's fine, Kelly. Take him to school. You know where I keep those little jars on the shelf downstairs. I have to get dinner." Mom went back to the kitchen.

Soon, Kelly was back. "Mom, I don't know how to catch him. What if he jumps?"

"I don't know. He might."

"But, Mom . . ."

"Your dad will be home soon. He can catch him."

"He might jump away by then."

"I guess he could." Mom turned the mixer back on.

"Mom!"

"*What*, Kelly?" Mom turned off the mixer.

"Help me. I want him."

"Kelly, it seems you're no braver about bugs than I am. And I don't want to get near him." The mixer went back on.

"Oh, Mom." Kelly left the room.

A few minutes later, Mom noticed Kelly sitting at the kitchen table looking at her katydid in a jar.

"Oh, you got him," Mom said, and went for a closer look.

"Donny got him for me," Kelly said without enthusiasm.

"That's good. That's what big brothers are for, I guess. I'm glad he didn't hop away first."

Kelly was silent a moment, then she said bitterly, "You didn't care. You wouldn't catch him."

At a moment when Kelly should be happy, she seems strangely dejected. What is the problem?

While the problem is perhaps partly Kelly's, let's focus on the portion that might be Mom's. We won't criticize her for her fear of insects, irrational though it is. The real problem is the feeling Kelly picked up that Mom wasn't interested, wasn't listening to her needs.

Had Mom known what Kelly was feeling, she could have taken time from her dinner preparations to help her daughter feel listened to. Kelly could have been helped to understand that she and her mom both share an aversion to catching insects. But she needed to feel heard. Otherwise, even when she got what she ostensibly wanted—a katydid in a jar—she would still feel that something was missing: her mother's love and willingness to help.

Hear My Real Problem

"You're old enough to decide if you want to go swimming, Jill." Dad was frustrated as he stood in his daughter's bedroom doorway. "I've said you could go, your chores are done, it's Saturday afternoon, you like to swim, you like Teri and Syd. There's really no reason *not* to go if *you* want to. I don't know what you want me to say."

"But, Dad," Jill began, "I . . ."

"It's just one of life's decisions, Jill. I'm not going to decide for you. You're nine years old. You decide."

Jill left the room in tears, and Dad went down the hall to find his wife. "I don't know what's wrong with that child," he said. "She can't decide *anything.*"

Later, Mom found Jill playing in her room. "What did you decide about swimming?" Mom asked.

"I didn't want to go."

"So you called and told them?"

"Yes."

Mom sat down on the bed and pulled Jill onto her lap. "Dad felt bad that you wanted him to decide for you. He wasn't being mean. He's just helping you learn to make decisions."

"That wasn't the problem, Mom," Jill protested. "I already knew I didn't want to go. When I was talking to Dad, I just wanted to know what to tell Teri. I kept saying 'What shall I say?' and Dad kept saying 'You'll have to decide.' I didn't want to be rude to my friends, and I didn't know what to tell them."

"So you didn't want help deciding whether to go?"

"No, I already knew that."

"I think I understand now, sweetheart. What did you tell them?"

Mom has read Jill's message correctly and discovered the real problem. Dad missed the point, perhaps because his preconception that Jill has a frequent problem in making decisions made him unable to hear what she was actually saying. Accurate though that observation may be, it wasn't the problem today. What Jill wanted wasn't advice on whether to go swimming but help on how to tell her friends, without hurting their feelings, that she didn't want to go.

Perhaps Dad didn't ask the right questions. Had he asked his daughter what she wanted to do, she would have said she didn't want to go. He could have then discovered the real problem, and the frustration on both sides would have been avoided. But without asking the right questions, Dad left Jill feeling unloved, or at least unlistened to—which is, after all, only a step behind unloved.

Teach Me About Spilt Milk

Dad had come home from a shopping trip in town and was hanging his coat in the hall closet when Jenny came in the door nearly in tears.

"Dad, look at this," she said.

"What is it, honey?"

"It's poster board and it's ruined."

"Oh?"

"I need it for school, and it's ruined."

Dad sat down on the stairs and pulled his daughter to his side. "It doesn't look too good, does it?" He held up the big sheet of heavy poster paper. A third of it was mangled and muddy. "What'd the other guy look like?"

When he saw his daughter wasn't in the mood for humor, he added, "Why don't you tell me about it?"

"There's a contest for sixth-graders to make posters about drugs—about not using drugs—and I wanted to do one, so I asked Mom for the money, and I went to the store to get this. On my way back, I was in front of Anderegg's house and I waved at Joey. It made my handlebars wobble and when I reached to grab them, a corner of the poster board caught in the spokes of my front tire. By the time I could yank it out, this is what happened."

Dad nodded and Jenny went on. "It cost fifty cents, and now it's ruined. Mom will be mad and won't want to give me more money."

Dad kissed his daughter's cheek. "Well," he said, "I'm sorry you feel bad, Jenny. But I've got an idea. You could make a poster that says, 'This is what your body will look like if you use drugs.'"

When Jenny rolled her eyes slightly, Dad said, "Just kidding! I've got an even better idea. I'll bet Mom can manage to come up with another half-dollar. Let's buy another piece of poster board and start over. Oh, I might have to take a second job or we might have to mortgage the house, but you're worth it!"

Dad has correctly read his daughter's concern and has responded appropriately. Her statement, "Mom will be mad and won't want to give me more money," is an indication that she expects to be blamed by her parents for the accident. And while parents have a right to teach care and caution when a child has clearly been irresponsible, there is also the equally important lesson of not crying over spilt milk.

Jenny will learn that accidents do happen, and that blame and reproach are often, at best, a waste of time and, at worst, needless guilt-producers destructive to a child's ego. At this point, soothing feelings and getting on with the task are the important things. When these occur, a child learns not only that most damages aren't irreparable but also the far more important lesson that she is loved and accepted and that her feelings are cared about.

I Need Time and Attention

Curt sat in his car at the traffic light on his way to work and suddenly realized what was troubling him. He'd been fretting all morning at some subconscious level and now he recognized that it was because of an incident from the previous evening with his sixteen-year-old son.

The family was at the dinner table when Tyler came out with a statement that really took Curt by surprise.

"You'll be glad," his boy said, "when we're all gone from home. Then you can do your own thing."

It was one of those comments that kind of came out without any real malice, and Curt recognized it as a reaction to his frequent Bill Cosby–style jokes, some of them in front of the kids, about being rid of them:

"Quick, the kids are outside—lock the doors!"

"Just think, dear, only eleven or twelve more years and we can use the bathroom and the car again."

"What did we ever do, honey, before we had these teenagers around to tell us how to do things?"

He hadn't thought much about Tyler's comment until this morning, when it came back to him with the realization that, to the children, these attempts at humor might not be seen as funny. Perhaps they actually didn't realize that his family meant everything to him and that he was really in no hurry to empty the nest.

As he drove on toward his office, he thought of two other incidents in the past week that had bothered him. One of them occurred when one of his children brought his school papers into the living room where Curt and his wife both sat. It was faintly disturbing to him when the child said, "Look, Mom, what I did in school today."

Maybe kids feel a greater affinity for their mothers at certain ages, Curt realized, but he had been sitting right there. Why had he needed to ask to be included?

The second incident was when his junior-high-school daughter had told her mom, but not Curt, about back-to-school night. When he learned of it from his wife and later asked Patti about it, she said innocently, "I didn't think you'd have time to come, Dad."

"I've always tried to attend your school affairs," he protested.

"I know, but I just didn't think about it. You can come."

Curt started to see a pattern, and he was worried.

Curt is faced with a potentially disturbing message from his children that they may not see him as very involved in their lives. It would be too simple to attribute it to lack of time, although his busy schedule may have contributed to the problem.

Curt is fortunate to have recognized the problem at this point when his children are still at home and when he can still turn things around.

Making the change needn't be difficult, although it will require effort and care. He can tell his children that his jokes about being "rid" of them are only jokes, and will stop. He can go out of his way to ask about school and other activities and homework. He can start conversations about his kids' interests and make an obvious attempt to listen. In a short time the children will feel appreciated by Dad, and he will start to again feel needed and included in their lives.

8

Help Me Be Me

A musical parent is alarmed to see her children showing no interest in practicing their scales. An athletic parent is worried when his son doesn't seem to enjoy the same sports he did.

Budding Beethovens don't spring from every parent who loves good music. Not every boy who cuts his teeth on a football grows up to be a star quarterback. Maybe he tries for a while, but his heart isn't in it. Football just isn't as important to him as it was to his father; he's more interested in duck hunting, playing the guitar, or tearing apart automobile transmissions.

What a surprise for us as parents to see our children striking out in different directions! Perhaps without giving it much thought, we assumed our children would follow pretty much the same path we ourselves took. But at some point we remember with a start that we ourselves didn't always follow the path of our own parents.

Occasionally we're reminded that raising children isn't much like raising sheep, after all. Each child has his or her own path to follow in development.

Certainly this doesn't mean we should not guide and teach—even at times cajole—our children. We would be poor parents indeed if we didn't *care* which path they took. But there is a vast difference between guiding and coercing, and the consequences of force are seldom good in the long run.

Our children often need our help to learn how best to pursue their ideal path, and the messages they send us often indicate this need. Our experience, offered with love, will help them learn who they are and where they want to go. Look at the following stories.

Motivate Me

"I read something today that really got me thinking about our kids," Dick said. He and Linda were planting seeds in their garden plot and having one of their regular discussions about family matters and parenting at the same time.

"Oh, what was that?" Linda asked.

"Well, a teacher was reporting on motivation in the classroom. One of the things he mentioned was that kids who say they enjoy a certain task—doing math, for instance—claim to enjoy it *less* when there's a reward attached to it."

"Oh?"

"Yes. He had students rate how well they enjoyed certain subjects and tasks in the classroom. Then he told those who rated math as a favorite subject they'd be allowed to do *less* of it for achieving high enough scores, and that they would also be given an external reward of some kind for doing well on their math. He again had them rate their interest after a while with this program. He found their enjoyment of math had gone down.

"Somehow, the reward had kind of ruined it—at least for those who already rated math as enjoyable. Maybe it told them they *shouldn't* be liking math for its own sake, or something. I don't know. But I wondered if the idea might apply to us and our family, say with our reward system for chores."

"We'd better look at the possibility," Linda said. "I noticed it's harder and harder to get Tim to do his practicing. I thought it was *in spite of* the rewards we came up with for each piece perfected. Maybe it was *because* of them!"

On the intuitive level, most parents are probably aware that the "eat-your-squash-and-you-can-have-some-ice-cream" motivator doesn't do much for a child's taste for squash.

As Dick has now learned, our reward system (often a bribe system) may lessen the enjoyment of other, ordinary tasks life requires of kids. And this has its dangers. We could probably make our children hate playing in the sunshine if we were to treat Vitamin D absorption as a duty!

Research shows that if we pay or otherwise reward our children for every job they have to do, whether household chores, homework, or skill practice, we may be unknowingly decreasing their interest in the task.

Certainly, we and our children do many things for various forms of reward. But a guiding principle for parents is this: If the internal reward (enjoyment of the job itself or the satisfaction of accomplishment) will suffice, let it. Don't add outside incentives that may become disincentives.

We must watch for those messages which will help us understand our children's motivation.

Accept My Differences

"Mom, we need to talk," Chelsea said, pulling her mom by the arm from the piano to a chair.

"OK," Mindy said. She never knew what this request would bring, coming from her vivacious fifteen-year-old, but the two had maintained a good mother-daughter relationship and they talked often.

"What's the deal?" she asked.

"It's about money," Chelsea said.

"Uh oh! You came to the wrong place for that. First Security is down the street."

"No, Mom," Chelsea laughed, "I'm not asking for any."

"Oh, she's *giving* today. Hey, everybody!" Mindy pretended to call down the hall, as if to the family. "Come on in. Chelsea's giving out money today."

"Not quite," Chelsea said, rolling her eyes.

"OK, honey. I see it's time to get serious here. What's the real question?"

"Well, you know how for years I've saved money to go to France on that NACEL exchange thing, like Varlene did years ago."

"Yes, I know. You were what, about ten, when she went? Let's see, she was seventeen, so you must have been nine or ten."

"Yes, I was ten. And it was exciting to see her off at the airport and pick her up a month later. She was so happy with the experience, and I decided right then, that's what I was going to do."

Mindy waited.

"Well," Chelsea said, "now that the time gets closer when I'd be old enough and have money enough to go, I . . . well, I don't know, it would be fun, I know, but . . . well, Varlene paid her own way, and . . ."

"Are you saying you don't want to spend your money on a French exchange?" Chelsea nodded slightly and Mindy went on. "Well, honey, that's OK. You seem like you're afraid to say so."

"Well, it's because I know we've talked about it for years, and Varlene thinks I'm going—she still mentions her trip a lot—and I didn't want to disappoint anybody, you know? I mean, it was such a big deal in Varlene's life. She even went on to major in French in college and everything."

Mindy gave her daughter a hug. "Hey, nobody is going to push you to go anywhere, especially when it's your own money you've saved. Don't worry about it. Everybody has different interests. Maybe you'll want to do something else with your money."

"Thanks, Mom." Chelsea cleared her throat. "You know, it's not that I don't want to go to France. It's just a matter of the money.

"That's the other thing I wanted to talk about—how I want to use my savings. You and Dad have had us save half of our money from the day we were born. So I don't know if I'm free to spend it how I want, or what. Is the money really mine, or is it only for big things like France or a mission or college? What if I'd just rather spend it on clothes and things?"

"Ah ha!" Mindy said. "Well, now, that's a different question. We'd better get your dad in on that one."

Chelsea's message is that she's no longer sure she wants to follow her older sister's footsteps in the use of her savings. Her mother is wise enough to let it be known that, while the question of a child's use of a full fifteen years of savings needs parental involvement, that's a different question from the main one—whether Chelsea is to be a clone of her sister. And Mindy has made it clear that Chelsea is free to seek her own paths.

Children *will* be different. One may go on a foreign exchange and take sky-diving lessons. Another may spend his money on tapes and records and camping equipment. Another may make his parents proud by earning a ham radio license and traumatize them by wanting to buy a motorcycle. But they *will* be different. It's their nature to want to "be me." Any parent who thinks his children will turn out just as he did, or just as he wants them to, must not have been a parent long.

While parents have a responsibility to advise, and even to arrange experiences they believe will be useful and helpful to growth and development, they must recognize when to step back and let divergent personalities take their various directions. Naturally, there will be instances where we wish certain things had gone the other way, but for the most part the diversity of our children should be a source of enjoyment for us, like sowing a package of mystery seeds and waiting to see what kinds of flowers spring up. Parents who see their children in this way will have many fewer disappointments.

Give Me Applause

"So, Martha, how are the reports today?" Ralph said as he sat down beside his neighbor in the line of parents waiting to talk with the junior high Spanish teacher.

"Oh, hi, Ralph. Well, let's put it this way—for a kid with a high IQ, J.D. seems to not want to let the information out! I have a feeling that if they had a trial to see if he had any smarts, there wouldn't be enough evidence to convict, he hides it so well."

Ralph smiled. "That's about what I'm hearing on Zack. I don't know how the kid manages to tell us his work is caught up, then we come here and have teachers tell us they haven't seen anything turned in all term." He shook his head. "Any ideas on how we can get these two to settle down?"

"Got any thumbscrews?" Martha smirked, before getting serious. "I don't know," she said, "whether having a smart older sister has made J.D. want to go the other way, or what. With Janelle getting the Sterling Scholar finalist award, it's not like he hasn't had a good example. I don't know—maybe we've praised her too much and made him feel like he couldn't keep up, so why try? I don't know."

"Yeah," Ralph said. "It's a tough one to figure out."

"We've tried to be conscious of comparisons and not compare or make J.D. feel he was of less value to us," Martha went on. "But we didn't feel it was fair not to praise Janelle for what she'd done, either. That wouldn't be right. But in scholastic matters, she's definitely received all the applause at our house."

At that moment the line moved forward and Martha went up to visit with Mr. Camron, leaving Ralph to wonder about her words and how they might apply in his own family. It was true that Zack's older brothers had done well in school and had been praised for it. Had this turned Zack in the other direction? Had he failed to receive the applause he needed in his chosen areas of excellence?

Ralph's questions are difficult and important ones. While he's not likely to come up with a fully satisfactory answer in the next five minutes, that doesn't make the matter less vital to consider. Clearly, how our children view themselves comes in part from how *they* perceive their parents view them. And part of this perception (or misperception) can come out of their feelings about how their parents view their siblings who achieve or don't achieve in areas important to the parents.

On the positive side, how many kids have made the wise decision to cause less trouble to their parents than they saw an older brother or sister cause? On the other hand, how many have felt they couldn't receive the applause or compete with the success of an older sibling, and so gave up trying? (And just because the parents didn't see it as a competition doesn't mean the child didn't.)

Applause. We all need it in one form or another, deadly, perverting intoxicant though it can be when excessive or unearned. The challenge is to find ways to provide esteem-building recognition in suitable areas for *each* child. If Zack and J.D. don't appear to be aiming at full scholarships to Harvard at this point in their lives, they each certainly still do well at *something*, even if that something is shoveling snow off the driveway or always saying "please" at the dinner table. Wise parents will make an effort to find and praise those things that are good.

And who knows? With increased self-esteem these two may decide they have the same scholarly capabilities as their older siblings. At a later time, perhaps after leaving the pinching, peer-enforced conformity of junior high school, they may surprise themselves and their parents by turning in an assignment on time, receiving a bit of applause for it, and coming to actually like the feeling. That's the message to watch for.

What About My Peers?

"I just can't understand it," Clare said. "Here I work with Kendall for days to memorize his little section of the Primary program, and he stands up there and *reads* it, like he's never seen it before. I don't know why they even let them have copies during the program, after they tell them to memorize their parts."

Clare and Tony were walking home from the ward Christmas party, where the Primary kids had put on a short program. Tony could tell from the speed with which his wife was striding that she was upset. He let her talk. The boys followed by several paces, and Clare kept her voice low.

"What a waste," she said. "It was so easy, too."

After a moment, Tony said, "You're probably right. I mean, I know Kendall knew his part, and he certainly could have repeated it, even though he seemed a little scared. But I noticed something. There were, let's see, eight kids in that line-up, spelling out the word C-H-R-I-S-T-M-A-S. No, nine. I watched carefully, since Kendall was first. What I observed was, all the boys read their parts and all the girls said theirs from memory."

"So?" Clare said. "Kendall still knew his; he didn't need to read it."

"I know," Tony said. "My guess is that the other boys, most of them, probably knew theirs too. There must be something about the age that kind of makes it normal, what we saw tonight.

"Notice, earlier, when they announced the older

youth were to come up and sing a couple of carols while we ate, not one boy went up, not one! The girls, all of them, as far as I could see, went up and sang, but no boys. In fact, I saw Zane glance over at us, and I think I read the message: 'No, Dad, don't push it.'

"I'm just saying, maybe our boys are about normal for their group. I'm not saying we couldn't ask more of the group—if as a church or as parents we decided to do so. But the way things are, our two might be about where they're supposed to be."

Peers and social influences. What a power they wield. Indirectly, maybe Tony is giving in to them as much as his boys are, by not pushing his boys to excel because others don't! On the other hand, maybe he's being realistic not to expect them—at certain ages, at least—to want to stand out too much from the crowd of other boys. The results of that aren't always good.

One who *always* expects more from his own child than the peer average can reap poor results as often as one who *never* does. In helping our children be themselves, we must factor in the peer group and read *their* messages, too.

Help Me Be My Best Me

Joshua awoke late Saturday morning and found a folded note by his bedside. He opened it and recognized his mom's handwriting. He read:

Dear Joshua:

I need to talk with you about a problem I've observed lately. I thought I'd put it in writing. You know I think you're a wonderful part of our family, and that your helpfulness and kindness to me, especially since your dad and I separated, have been a source of joy to me. I very much enjoy you as you are, and I hope what I have to say won't hurt your feelings.

But there is something causing me concern as I see it affecting our family and your relationship with your younger brothers and sisters. It's this: you seem to have adopted a tone of judgment and harshness with many of their actions. I'll give you some examples of what I mean. Night before last, when Jana's little friend was here, you said something cutting about her staying for dinner. She may or may not have heard it, and you may have only meant it as a joke, but it sounded rude. Last week in family home evening, when I said we needed to talk about family chores, you muttered something like, "Oh, so Ben's not doing his work again." Now, you may have meant it to be funny, but I didn't see your brother act like he enjoyed it.

Joshua, you have a unique style of handling problems, with your light way of responding and cooling things down. This is marvelous, and we've praised you for your approach many times. It has gotten us through many difficult situations, and has often been very funny, too. We love it! Don't change it! But lately, I've seen this other kind of speaking creeping in, and it kind of spoils things.

I don't want you to stop being you, Josh. I only want you to be your *best you.*

Love, Mom

Joshua is sending a message that needs correction. Whether he will understand and respond to his mother's concern remains to be seen, but her message to him is a vital one: it's great to be funny, clever, and able to smooth rough situations.

Joshua will learn that the line between pleasant repartee and cutting invective is fairly thin. But when it is crossed, the responses engendered in others are completely different. The one comes across as a smile, the other as a snarl.

Television and movie humor often thrives on put-downs and cut-lows, and it's natural for our kids to pick up the method. They need to learn that in real life the results are not usually as funny as scripted. Such a lesson is an important step in helping our kids learn to be themselves—but their *best* selves.

As parents, our biggest task is to help our children reach their potential. We must allow them the right to be themselves, but by our guidance and love and our attention to the messages they send us we can help them be their best selves.